MASTERING
THE TEACHING
OF ADULTS

By
Jerold W. Apps
Professor, Adult/Continuing Education
University of Wisconsin-Madison

KRIEGER PUBLISHING COMPANY
MALABAR, FLORIDA

This book is the result of a joint venture between Krieger Publishing Company, Malabar, Florida, and LERN (Learning Resources Network), Manhattan, Kansas.

Original Edition 1991

Printed and Published by
KRIEGER PUBLISHING COMPANY
KRIEGER DRIVE
MALABAR, FLORIDA 32950

Library of Congress Cataloging-In-Publication Data
Apps, Jerold W., 1934-
    Mastering the teaching of adults / Jerold W. Apps.—Original ed.
        p.   cm.
    Includes bibliographical references (p.) and index.
    ISBN 0-89464-558-7 (alk. paper)
    1. Adult education teacher—Training of —United States. 2. Adult education—Study and teaching—United States. .I. Title.
    LC5225.T4A69 1991
    370'.71'2—dc20   91-3362
                                                                            CIP

10   9   8   7   6   5   4   3

MASTERING THE
TEACHING
OF ADULTS

CONTENTS

Contents

OTHER BOOKS BY JEROLD W. APPS

Toward a Working Philosophy of Adult Education
Redefining the Discipline of Adult Education (With R. Boyd)
Problems in Continuing Education
The Adult Learner on Campus
Study Skills for Adults Returning to School
Study Skills for Today's College Student
Instructor's Manual: Study Skills for Today's College Student
Improving Your Writing Skills
How To Improve Adult Education in Your Church
Ideas for Better Church Meetings
Improving Practice in Continuing Education
Higher Education in a Learning Society
The Land Still Lives
Cabin in the Country
Village of Roses
Skiing Into Wisconsin: A Celebration of Winter
Barns of Wisconsin
Mills of Wisconsin and the Midwest

ACKNOWLEDGMENTS

Much of what I've learned about teaching adults comes from the hundreds of students I've taught over the years in settings ranging from cold one-room country schools heated with wood stoves to graduate school seminar rooms. I want to acknowledge and express my heartfelt thanks to all these people who put up with my constant experimentation with new teaching approaches—and who helped me sort out what worked from what didn't.

I am also indebted to the researchers and scholars who have studied adults, adult learning, and teaching. I have used their writings extensively in my work and in the writing of this book.

A special thank you to William Draves, executive director of the Learning Resources Network. Bill has long recognized the importance of good teaching and outstanding teachers in adult education, and he encouraged me to share my experiences and thoughts on these topics.

Several people read the manuscript and offered suggestions for improvement. I particularly want to thank Keith Iddings, for his interest and understandings about ethics in adult education; Judy Adrian, for her attention to the practical; and Rob Domaingue, who knows the power of the story and the challenge to make writing readable as well as useful. Sue Horman, a second grade teacher in Columbus, Ohio and also my daughter read the manuscript and asked often, "What do you mean here, Dad?" To all these people and many more, I owe a great debt.

CHAPTER 1

Introduction

In this book I emphasize an approach to teaching adults where you, the teacher, engage your entire personality, how you think, what you know and how you know it, and how you feel and why you feel that way. I emphasize a teaching approach that involves all of the learner, too—feelings, thoughts, relationships, backgrounds, values, beliefs—everything that makes a person unique.

As a teacher of adults you can recognize and applaud what a person already knows and build on it rather than concentrate on a person's deficiencies. You can listen carefully to what people say they want to learn, but you ought not stop there. Most learners want to be challenged to see beyond their immediate wants and needs. As a teacher, you ought be prepared to help learners understand the meaning of what they are learning, help them explore and create, and help them critically analyze as well as think introspectively.

You are empowering learners by helping them take charge of their own learning, by helping them learn how to learn and assisting them to become comfortable with the process. And probably most important of all, your teaching can challenge learners to reach beyond their wildest dreams for achievement, helping them to soar to new heights and accomplishments. The poet Guillaume said it well:

> Come to the edge, he said.
> They said: we are afraid.
> Come to the edge, he said.
> They came.
> He pushed them . . . and they flew.

This book will show you how to teach from the perspective described above, but before moving into some of the particulars, here are a few reasons why this highly personal approach to teaching adults will be so important in the years ahead.

1

DEMAND FOR CONTINUAL LEARNING

Most careers these days demand that workers constantly learn. Long gone is the old idea that you prepare for a career, you do it, and you retire. Most of us are constantly learning in our jobs, every day.

I was talking with a trainer in a major electronics corporation recently. He told me that in order to compete with foreign manufacturers of electronic products, his company must design a new product, manufacture, and market it in one year. Imagine the pressure on the trainers, and on the workers who must quickly learn many new techniques. Not only must we all keep on learning, but for many of us economic competition has speeded up the process and made time an important element to consider.

Computers have forever changed how we think of time and, as a result, how we think about ourselves and everything around us. Computers operate with nanoseconds (a billionth of a second). We cannot experience a nanosecond—it's simply too fast. Snap your finger. More than 500 million nanoseconds have passed.

A backlash is resulting from the pressures of time and the demands to learn more, faster. Occasionally it may be necessary, in the spirit of global competition, to learn something quickly—particularly if it is a new skill. But most business leaders these days recognize the need to employ people who can think creatively and critically. Increasingly employers want workers who can think as well as perform.

Those adult learners caught up in speed learning thirst for opportunities to be more deliberate, to think about ideas more deeply, to see broader implications and wider applications. As teachers, we must be prepared to respond. The response means mastering how to teach in a highly personal way.

Lifelong learning goes well beyond the workplace. Adults want to learn for personal enjoyment as well as for economic gain. They want to gain new appreciation for the arts and seek new understandings of literature, history, geography, and a host of other topics. They are concerned about their physical and mental health. For the in-depth learning that most adults demand, a personal approach to teaching is the most appropriate one.

Lifelong learning also includes a consideration of global issues such as social, economic, and environmental problems with community, state, national, and international applications. The teaching approach I am advocating leads to empowerment of adult learners which in turn can lead to improved communities, strengthened democratic institutions, and the solving of social problems.

INFORMATION PARALYSIS

Information is doubling every four or five years. We are literally awash in information, bits and pieces of facts, row upon row of numbers, report after report of research and survey findings. Some of the information is accurate, some false, some applies to our lives, most of it does not.

We find hundreds of thousands of people literally paralyzed by information. Someone has told them they must keep up or they'll become obsolete. So they read, attend lectures, watch videotapes, and listen to audio tapes in their cars as they drive to work. Information pours over them.

Some say that the more information we accumulate, the better our lives will be. For many people, the more information they have, the more paralyzed they become. Their entire personal information system locks up and refuses to budge.

As a teacher, here's where you can help. Adults experiencing information paralysis want you to help them make sense out of the information they have before you provide them with more. They don't need more information choices.

They look to you, the teacher, to help them find their way through the thicket of facts and the morass of competing perspectives. They want you to help them decide what information fits their questions and problems. They want some help in deciding which information is accurate and which is not. Many want to learn how to examine information critically, so that they really understand it from their own perspectives. Most learners already know far more than they think they know. You can help them become aware of and appreciate this personal knowledge.

Likewise, you can assist learners in knowing what they don't know. Once they have done this, they will often look to you to help them acquire the specific information they need.

INFORMATION TECHNOLOGY

Two major developments in technology during the past decade are greatly influencing adult learning: (1) how information is stored and retrieved and (2) how information is transmitted.

Almost unlimited information is available in various electronic forms. Optically scanned information storage systems such as Compact Disk Read Only Memory (CD-ROM) provide adult learners quick access to information. Many libraries have research information available in this form. One CD-ROM disk will hold the equivalent of 250,000 pages of information, which is the equivalent of a small library. Books are available on audio tape, as are many other kinds of information. Video tapes provide information on innumerable topics.

The means by which information can be transmitted have become increasingly more sophisticated, including the use of satellites to send video images, fax machines for short messages, computer electronic mail systems, and so on.

As you read this, some new approach to storing, retrieving, and delivering information is likely coming on the market. This has several implications for the adult learner and for you, the teacher of adults. First, as teacher you are no longer the sole or even the major provider of information for adult learners, in most situations. Second, as teacher, you will be increasingly asked to help adult learners become "information literate." This means assisting learners in matching information to their questions and problems, helping them judge which information to discard and which to keep, helping them critically think about information, and of course helping them acquire information from many sources including the electronic ones.

FOR THE TEACHER OF ADULTS

Most of the examples used in the book will be for those of you who work face to face with groups, which is where it is easiest to apply a personal teaching approach. These groups may include older or younger adults interested in learning everything from creative writing to carpentry, from recreational skills to world politics, from Chaucer to Steinbeck, from job related skills to parenting.

As a teacher of adults you may work full time or part time. Your employer may be a business or an industry, a community recreation department, a public school, a college or university extension division, a church, a health facility, a community organization such as Red Cross or the YWCA, a labor union or the military, a library or a museum, a consulting firm, or you may be in business for yourself as a provider of educational opportunities. I assume that you have had some experience teaching adults. This book is designed to build on that experience.

When I think about teaching adults, I am often reminded of this story. A tourist visiting a large city saw several bricklayers working on a church. She could see that it was a very large church and she was curious. Coming up to a bricklayer she asked, "What are you doing?"

Without looking up the bricklayer growled, "You can plainly see that I'm laying bricks."

The tourist watched for awhile, observing how the bricklayer placed a layer of mortar, and carefully positioned each brick making sure it was straight and true. One after the other the bricklayer placed the bricks, almost machine-like. He seldom looked up, never smiled.

The tourist moved around the building and met a second bricklayer. He seemed to be following the same procedures as the first bricklayer. Except he was humming a song as he worked.

"What are you doing?" the tourist asked the second bricklayer. She thought she knew what she would hear, but she asked anyway.

"I'm building a cathedral," the second bricklayer said proudly, a smile spreading across his sun-tanned face. "I'm building a cathedral."

This book is about teaching adults, not about laying bricks and building cathedrals—but there is a resemblance between teaching and bricklaying. Both bricklayers and teachers can do acceptable work with well-developed skills. But to be masters, both need something more than basic skills. The second bricklayer had an attitude of greatness—that he was contributing to something that was important and that made a difference. He was more than *merely* a person laying bricks. Likewise, master teachers have a vision for what they hope to accomplish—a vision that stretches into the future and transcends the day-to-day work that must be done. *Master teachers are helping build cathedrals in the minds of the learners with whom they work.*

CHAPTER 2

You Know More Than You Think

You know more about teaching adults than you think you know. Below are two ways of finding out what you know. For some of you, the first approach—Telling Your Story—will be the most revealing. Others of you will find the Master Checklist helpful, not only in assessing your knowledge, but in helping you decide where to improve. Completing both exercises, Telling Your Story and the Master Checklist, will help you develop a more comprehensive and multileveled understanding of your abilities.

EXERCISE 1—TELLING YOUR STORY

Your stories can be the windows to discovering what you know about teaching, what teaching adults means to you, and the kinds of feelings teaching evokes. Your stories can also help you become aware of how much you already practice the teaching approaches described in this book.

Try this simple exercise. Think back to a teaching experience after which you felt particularly good. This could be an adult class you recently taught. It could be a workshop session, a seminar, or perhaps even something you did that is much more informal—but you would describe it as teaching.

First, write a description of the situation including as much detail as you can remember. What time of day was it? Anything unusual about the weather? Picture the facilities. Describe the room. How was it arranged, and what kind of feeling did it give you? Characterize the subject matter or the topic you were teaching. Describe the participants. Ages? Your impressions of them? Their level of interest? Anyone that seemed always to disagree with you? What teaching approaches did you use? How did you involve the participants, assuming that you did? What overall comments would you make about the situation? Beyond describing the detail of a teaching situation, it sometimes helps to describe it in global terms.

Next, sit back and reflect for a moment. Why did you feel good about this teaching situation? Write down your thoughts.

Now look back at your description of the situation. Why did it work well? What did you do that worked especially well? Did some approaches seem to work better than others? Consider how you organized the subject matter, any handouts you may have used, the teaching approaches you followed, how you interacted with learners, and so on.

Did you have difficulty listing everything you did that seemed to make a difference? Most teachers simply don't know everything that makes a difference in their teaching.

Describe, if you can, in whatever words you want to use, some of these intangibles that made a difference in this teaching situation. Sometimes one specific event makes the difference for an entire session—how you responded to a particular learner's question, for example. Other times a kind of cumulative effect comes into play; one thing builds on another and the group seems to come alive and respond. These intangibles are often what makes the difference between a "so-so" performance and outstanding teaching. They comprise some of the art of excellent teaching, but are difficult to explain, just as an artist may not be able to describe fully the process of creating a work of art.

Though creativity has elements of mystery in it, artists must have a series of definable skills and understandings to create art. A knowledge of color, of paint and brushes, and of perspective and shapes is a basic part of the process of becoming an outstanding artist. Of course this knowledge and these skills alone are clearly not enough to produce art.

Likewise, you must have certain knowledge and skills that are basic to teaching. Such knowledge and skills alone, though, do not make for outstanding teaching. The intangible dimension is what ultimately makes the difference between average teaching and exceptional teaching.

EXERCISE 2—THE MASTER CHECKLIST

I have developed the Master Checklist, as shown in Figure 2.1, based on many years of teaching adults.

There are some cautions in using the checklist. If you are a relative newcomer to teaching adults you may look at this list, slam the book shut, and say, "I can never do all those things." I agree. You certainly can't

MASTER CHECKLIST

Place a check mark in the appropriate column for each item. Check "0" if you believe you do not have this quality, competency, or characteristic. Check "4" if you believe you have this quality, competency, or characteristic at a high level.

		0	1	2	3	4
1.	Clear about purpose for teaching	__	__	__	__	__
2.	Know personal teaching style	__	__	__	__	__
3.	Know how to overcome adult learning myths	__	__	__	__	__
4.	Can use a broad array of teaching tools	__	__	__	__	__
5.	Know how to select teaching tools for particular purposes and situations	__	__	__	__	__
6.	Know characteristics of adults as learners, and can apply this knowledge	__	__	__	__	__
7.	Can organize content for teaching	__	__	__	__	__
8.	Aware of and know how to assess quality in teaching and learning	__	__	__	__	__
9.	Can make ethical decisions	__	__	__	__	__
10.	Can teach critical thinking skills	__	__	__	__	__
11.	Have a basis for teaching	__	__	__	__	__

My Master Teaching score is _____ out of a possible 44.

Figure 2.1

know and be able to do immediately everything on the list—nor should you even consider it. The list is a guide for examining what you now do well, and a starting place for thinking about how you can improve. Also, no universal teaching prescription fits all adult learners in all learning situations. Ronald Cervero (1988), professor of adult education at the University of Georgia, reminds us that teachers of adults "work in a variety of different situations that make radically different demands on their skills, knowledge and judgment. . . . each [teaching] principle means different things and emerges as different practices in varying contexts" (p. 151).

A key to becoming a master teacher is the ability to adjust your teaching strategies to different situations, to varying learner needs, to demands of different subject matter and so on. Teacher characteristics such as enthusiasm, caring for others, ability to listen, and knowledge of subject matter would seem to transcend most teaching situations.

Keep your Master Teaching score for future reference. Sometime later, you may want to return to the checklist and complete it again, noting changes.

After completing the Telling Your Story and the Master Checklist exercises, you should have quite a good idea of where you stand in your progress toward becoming a master teacher. You are probably surprised at how much you already know.

CHAPTER 3

Taking Charge of Your Teaching

My first job teaching adults was for the University of Wisconsin Extension Service. I remember those first few months when my supervisor, concerned that I got off to a good start, insisted that I conduct my workshops in exactly the way he suggested. He told me how to organize what I was to teach, what teaching methods I should use, even how I should stand in front of a group—in fact, I was merely a clone of him. In some ways it was a comfortable situation. I didn't have to think much about what I was doing. I merely had to follow directions and to perform.

It wasn't long, though, until I began to feel extremely frustrated. I knew some teaching approaches outside my supervisor's repertoire, and I wanted to try them. I didn't appreciate the lockstep way in which he wanted me to organize what I was teaching. I had some ideas of my own.

For one evening's class, I decided to do what I wanted to do in the way in which I wanted to do it. I knew I was taking a risk. Information about whether what I did worked or didn't work would soon filter back to my supervisor and I would hear about it. I went ahead, with perspiration beading my forehead.

About twenty youth leaders were in the workshop—I was teaching a session on how to organize and run youth groups. I remember being a bit hesitant at first. I was doing what I wanted to do in the way in which I wanted to do it, but I also had no experience following my own lead.

The two-hour session sped by. When it was over I felt good, although some parts of the session were clearly rough and needed more polish. Three people came up to me afterward. "Where did this Jerry Apps come from?" one of them said. A broad smile spread across her face. "Bring him along with you to our next session."

From that moment I began to take charge of my own teaching. I must quickly add how much I appreciated my supervisor's concern for my success and acknowledge that I learned much from him about how to teach adults, what to teach, and what not to do. But I felt so much better

11

about me and about my teaching when I was in charge of what I was doing. That is not to say that I was always right. Indeed not. I have made my share of mistakes and committed more gaffes than anyone ought, but they were mine and I took responsibility for them.

In many situations you may feel powerless; you feel that others control your teaching and you are merely a conduit, a vehicle for other people's decisions and actions. You come to a teaching assignment, no matter if you are a literacy teacher in a technical college or a trainer in business, with the feeling that you are but one small cog in a massive teaching machine.

Maxine Greene (1978), a writer in education, argues that too many teachers, from the public schools on through various forms of adult teaching, are dominated by administrators and bureaucracy. She says teachers, particularly those who have a "purely technical training or a simplified 'competency based' approach, . . . are likely to see themselves as mere transmission belts—or clerks" (p.38).

It is easy to allow the stresses of the job and the pressures of living to consume you so that you have no time to look, listen, and reflect on what is happening around you. You become a slave to calendars and schedules, to deadlines and appointments. You may lose sight of where you are and who you are within it all.

Taking charge of your teaching doesn't mean ignoring the suggestions of supervisors and administrators. Taking charge of your teaching means being a partner, not a powerless actor. It means expressing ideas and trying new approaches. It means standing up for what you believe. Taking charge of your teaching means keeping in touch with yourself, your thoughts and feelings about teaching and about your life as a teacher, and it means questioning your own assumptions about what you are doing and questioning the assumptions of the organization for which you work.

In addition to making decisions about what you will teach and how you will teach it, taking charge of your teaching includes taking responsibility for your personal learning and self-improvement, including accepting the need to often unlearn certain attitudes and skills and knowledge. Let's now turn to each of these tasks.

RESPONSIBILITY FOR PERSONAL IMPROVEMENT

One important dimension of taking charge of your teaching is to take charge of your own learning—to keep up with both the subject matter you teach and the ways in which you teach it.

Just as you may sometimes depend on others to tell you what to teach and how to teach it, you may also depend on in-service opportunities to keep you up-to-date. Map out your *own* professional improvement plan. In most instances such a plan will include the in-service opportunities your organization, agency, or institution makes available, but it will usually go well beyond such opportunities. You can design your own reading plan, your own set of contact people to consult when you have a question or problem, and your own travel schedule that will enrich your life.

In my judgment, teachers really can't take charge of their teaching until they've taken charge of their own self-improvement.

UNLEARNING

Another aspect of taking charge of your own teaching is learning how to give up old habits, old ideas, old attitudes, and old ways of thinking.

When I first began teaching, everything was based on behavioral objectives. You decided what behavioral changes you wanted the learner to achieve—either a change in knowledge, a change in skills, or a change in attitude. Many of my early in-service training sessions included specific directions on how to write behavioral objectives: they must focus on the learner, they must include action verbs, and they must be specific enough so learning results can be measured.

After my first five years of teaching I began to feel quite confident, even a little smug, that I had this teaching business all figured out. All I had to do was write specific behavioral objectives and all would be well.

From time to time, though, as the years passed, I discovered that behavioral objectives didn't fit well in every situation. I remember so vividly when I began teaching writing at the Rhinelander School of Arts in Rhinelander, Wisconsin. The poet-in-residence sniffed when I began telling her about the behavioral objectives I had been following in my writing classes, and how I planned to measure the results of my teaching efforts.

"How do you measure the extent someone is drawing on his or her creativity? How do you measure the extent you are contributing to the celebration of the human spirit?"

I tried to answer but soon discovered I hadn't thought about behavioral objectives in an artistic situation. So I withdrew, at first becoming defensive and later wanting to reject the poet's comments with a "what could she know about teaching, she's only a poet."

But those questions nagged at me, more than I thought they would.

I could understand the excitement of creative expression and the human spirit. In my own way I was trying to evoke such tendencies in my writing classes. As I thought about the questions and reflected on my own teaching style, I began to see that I was trying to teach writing in quite a technical, near mechanical way. I finally concluded that to the extent that I used a technical approach (behavioral objectives, etc.) I prevented some creative expression. This insight hit me hard.

Not only did I begin to think about the inadequacy of behavioral objectives for my writing classes, I began to wonder about my carte blanche use of behavioral objectives for all my teaching. What was happening to me?

I was experiencing the beginning of the unlearning process. Unlearning means we have to set aside a way of thinking and doing that we thought appropriate. In fact, the most difficult things to unlearn are those ways of thinking and doing that we hold most dear—in my case, behavioral objectives.

Very often we don't have an alternative way of thinking and doing. If not behavioral objectives, then what? Becoming aware that unlearning is necessary is one phase in the process. In some ways this can be the most unnerving, for long standing beliefs and practices are called into question.

Once we have accepted that our way of thinking and doing may no longer be appropriate, we search for alternatives. In this instance, I began talking with the poet to see how she taught and what sort of expectations she had for her teaching. I read everything I could find on alternative teaching approaches and did considerable thinking about what I had been doing in light of this information.

Soon I began to see alternatives, but accepting them would mean rather substantial changes in how I taught. The question now was, did I want to do this? I was in the transition phase of unlearning.

Sometimes it's necessary to completely give up old ways of thinking and doing as a part of the transition phase of unlearning. In doing so, we may very well mourn the loss of what is familiar and comfortable, and this mourning process may take some time.

Occasionally we may expand our horizons; the behavioral objective situation for me is an example. I did not give up behavioral objectives, but I did learn when to apply them and when not to. I gave up the belief that behavioral objectives applied in every situation. Another phase of unlearning is applying the new learning—the new way of thinking and doing.

As we strive to become master teachers, we will often face situations that challenge our ways of doing things. Often, before we can go on, we must face up to the unlearning and work through the process. The old idea, the old attitude, the old way of doing may be blocking our progress. Until we set it aside, until we unlearn, we are thwarted.

The period of reflection described above usually provides the first step—an awareness that some unlearning is necessary. Recording unlearning episodes in a journal provides a means for assisting the unlearning process, including recording the strong feelings the process usually evokes.

JOURNAL WRITING

Many years ago I began writing in a journal, first using a loose-leaf notebook and later a hard cover book with blank pages. I've found journal writing an extremely powerful tool not only for helping me get in touch with my teaching, but also for confronting myself. I try to write something every day. Some days it may be only a report of what I did the previous day: if I was teaching, what the topic was, and something about the learners. Other days I go much further.

Some of the ways journal writing has helped me take charge of my teaching include the following.

To name and clarify my teaching. By writing about my teaching, including the details of relationships with learners, the frustrations with facilities, the challenges of working with ever-changing content, I am able to clarify my thoughts, feelings, and observations about my teaching. Journal writing allows me to explore the interplay between my concrete experiences and the abstract thoughts I have about them, thereby strengthening the power and precision of my thinking.

To discover unknowns about how I teach. I often become aware of new dimensions of my teaching. All of us know more about teaching than we are conscious of. Our body language, how we respond to questions, knowing when to switch to a new topic, approaches for encouraging the timid and dampening the over-aggressive—all are techniques we use subtly and sometimes without awareness. Writing can help us begin to uncover these unknown skills, although certain aspects of our teaching, I firmly believe, can never be put into words.

To define and solve problems. Sometimes problems emerge in our classes and we are baffled about what to do. I remember so clearly the second session of a semester-long class of thirty-five participants. A tall, blond haired young man in his early thirties stood up, looked me in the eye, and asked, "When are you going to teach us something, I mean really teach something? I've had it with your questions and stories." I let it pass, thanking him for his contribution while trying hard not to sound defensive. That night, when I wrote in my journal, I talked about the class and what I had been doing and how the learners were reacting. And of course I talked about the young man who had rather belligerently confronted me. I wrote about alternative actions I might take. I could change my teaching approach. I could talk with him before class and try to explain what I was trying to do with my teaching. I could take time to try to explain to the entire class what I was doing and why. I tried writing about this young man from his perspective, as well as I could, trying to place myself in his shoes. And then I decided to do nothing. I'll never really know if that was the right decision, but journal writing helped me crawl into the problem and look in all the corners, some of them dark and difficult to understand. At the next session, the young man seemed more settled and accepting, and I went on, following the same approach I had followed in earlier sessions.

To create new ideas. The process of journal writing often becomes a highly creative activity for me as new ideas, new connections, new ways of doing old things, old ways of doing new things, pop into my mind and I write them down. Thus writing becomes not only a way to express creativity, but a trigger for creativity itself.

To clarify personal values. As I write and attempt to clarify my thoughts about teaching, I of course must make choices because I can't write about everything. Thus, in a very practical way, I am coming to grips with what is most important to me. I am, in effect, identifying my values.

To provide a historical record. I record the titles of books I have read, meetings I attended, names and addresses of people I have been in touch with, and a host of other "historical" information. My journal thus becomes a invaluable record in addition to the other ways journal writing has assisted me.

I would encourage you to try journal writing. I've found it an extremely useful tool for helping me take charge of my teaching.

CHAPTER 4

Myths About Teaching Adults

As I think back, several myths about teaching adults have blocked many teachers from doing their best work. I know from time to time they've gotten in my way.

MYTH ONE: IN NEARLY EVERY WAY TEACHING ADULTS DIFFERS FROM TEACHING CHILDREN.

Because of this myth, researchers, scholars, and writers involved with adult learning have paid little attention to the research and practice occurring in the public schools. Many assume that the public schools continue to follow a heavily lecture-oriented teaching approach with little or no learner involvement.

In fact, the public schools, in most instances, have redefined what "teacher" means and what teachers do. Indeed, we can learn much from teachers working today in elementary and secondary education. Many of these teachers involve learners in extremely creative ways; they incorporate educational technology in an interesting manner, and they work toward applying what learners learn to real life situations. Unfortunately a more enlightened teaching approach is often less evident at the college and university level where many teachers cling to eighteenth century teaching approaches. But even here we are beginning to see fresh teaching approaches, with instructors challenging learners to think about and apply what they are learning.

MYTH TWO: WHAT TEACHERS DO IS DIRECTLY TIED TO WHAT LEARNERS LEARN.

Some teachers apply a scientific efficiency model to teaching. Such language as inputs and outputs, learners as products, behavioral objectives, performance indicators for teachers, and the like are demonstrations of this myth.

Some teachers of adults have been misled in believing that social and behavioral researchers will eventually discover a set of scientific rules that teachers can follow. The thinking goes like this: if I follow teaching method "A" then learning "X" will result. The idea of basing teaching approaches on "solid scientific research" has been around for a long time. Experienced teachers have found again and again that such research, although helpful for certain kinds of tasks and for certain types of learners, usually fails to provide overall guidelines for teaching. Human beings simply do not react uniformly to teaching approaches, and thus common teaching strategies often result in multiple results (Tom, 1984, pp. 41–54).

Teaching includes elements of applied science and art. Applied science can help inform teaching, but artful strategies also strongly influence what successful teachers do.

MYTH THREE: WE CAN IDENTIFY A TECHNOLOGY OF TEACHING.

A technology of teaching generally includes assessing needs, writing learner objectives, selecting appropriate teaching approaches, and designing evaluation strategies. We can readily find such prescriptions for teachers of adults in the literature. Unfortunately, these prescriptions leave the impression that they are the only way to teach adults, with no suggestion of flexibility. In reality, in some situations a needs assessment may not be appropriate; in other situations carefully developed learner objectives may thwart learning; and preplanned, narrowly developed evaluation schemes may miss the most important learning that actually takes place.

MYTH FOUR: TEACHERS ARE BORN NOT MADE.

MYTH FIVE: ONLY THOSE TEACHERS WITH PROPER TEACHING CREDENTIALS SHOULD BE ALLOWED TO TEACH.

These myths are paired because, although we often hear both of them, seldom do we realize that they contradict each other. Myth four assumes that you either have what it takes to be a teacher or you don't. No training and experience will make any difference. Myth five assumes that training is what makes all the difference, particularly that training which leads to tangible evidence that you've studied teaching—such as a degree or certificate.

An element of truth exists in both these myths. It certainly helps to be born with a good speaking voice, ample energy, and good health. On the other hand, this book is proof that we believe we can improve ourselves by reading and listening and reflecting on our experiences. Unfortunately, there are those who want to prevent good teachers from teaching because they don't have the credentials. In my years of experience I have seen hundreds of noncredentialed teachers of adults doing outstanding jobs. Some of them work full time, some part time, and some volunteer their services. I have also seen credentialed teachers who failed miserably when actually teaching. In addition, you and I both have seen miserable performances by noncredentialed teachers and quite exemplary performances from those with certificates. I am quite convinced that additional information and training can assist teachers to become better teachers, but the credential alone does not make the difference between good and bad teaching.

MYTH SIX: TEACH WHAT THE LEARNERS WANT TO BE TAUGHT.

This idea grew out of the consumer movement and the belief that consumers always know best what they want and need. Those of us in education were led to believe that successful businesses always started with what customers said they wanted.

Recently I read an interview with Steve Jobs, the founder of Apple Computer. Jobs said he doesn't ask potential customers what they want. By the time you have it ready for them they'll want something else. Jobs believes, as a businessman, that you have to be ahead of the customers. "It seems logical to ask customers what they want and then give it to them. But they rarely wind up getting what they really want that way" ("Entrepreneur," 1989).

MYTH SEVEN: TEACHING SHOULD ALWAYS FOCUS ON INDIVIDUALS AND THEIR PROBLEMS AND NEEDS.

True, much teaching does and probably should be individually oriented. But there are two problems when we focus only on individual learner problems and needs. First, not all learning should begin with some discrepancy—some problem or need. Often learners want to build on strengths, to start with their strong points and build on them rather than start with their shortcomings and try to overcome them. In other words, we should more often start with what learners know, not what they don't know.

Also, by solely focusing on teaching individuals, whether building on strengths or solving individual problems, we ignore larger community and global problems. Some people firmly believe that we will solve community problems, say solid waste disposal problems, concern for energy conservation, or pesticide contamination of food by teaching individuals about these problems. Others believe that we solve community problems by the social action or community development approach to teaching. True, individuals involved in this process learn much. The focus, however, is not on their individual learning, but on the problem itself and its solution in the community.

Examining where you stand in reference to each of these myths is a major step toward improving yourself as a teacher, for these myths often lurk in the background, deterring you from becoming what you can become.

CHAPTER 5

Thinking as a Teacher

I was talking recently with a wood carver who carved wild ducks and other wild birds.

"Tell me how you go about this," I asked him.

"Well," he began, as he fondled a block of wood and chuckled softly, "I start with the belief that there's a duck hidden in this block of wood and it's my job to find it."

As he talked he turned the block of coarse wood this way and that, running his long slim fingers over the grain and allowing the light to play on the texture and color.

"Do you always find the duck?"

"Nope, sometimes it ain't in there. I'd thought it was, but it wasn't. Mostly though, I find the duck. When I go looking for it I usually find it."

I asked him to tell me more about the process he used.

"It's hard to talk about," he said. "But you're welcome to watch."

He began with a saw, cutting out the rough shape of a duck and then he proceeded with a series of knives to whittle away at the block.

"How long does it take to carve a duck?" I asked after fifteen minutes or so of watching.

The old carver looked up at me, a sly smile spread across his wrinkled face. "Takes a lifetime to carve a duck," he said. "Takes a lifetime."

He went on to explain that everything that happened to him over the years, his love for the outdoors, his upbringing near a wildlife marsh, his hunting trips with his father—all influenced how he carved a duck. "And of course some years of practice with these," he said as he pointed to his collection of knives.

As he carved and we talked, I began to understand more about what he meant by a lifetime of investment in his craft. He clearly was putting his entire person into his carving projects. As he worked he slowly turned the wood, looking at it, running his craggy fingers over the surface, re-

21

moving a sliver of wood here, another sliver there. He told me he constantly thought of past ducks he'd carved, and how this one was the same but always different—so he was always drawing on his experience and also doing things he'd never done before.

"You know," he said, not looking up from the wood block. "A computer can carve a duck—in not much time either. But they all look the same—they are the same—one duck just like every other duck. But the ducks I carve are unique to the block of wood that gives them birth. I take into account the nuances in wood grain, and the knots, and the changes in hardness and softness of the wood. I'm constantly adjusting, constantly trying something new."

He allowed several wood slivers to drop to the floor before continuing. "Much of what I do, the particular cuts I make, the way I hold a particular knife to achieve a given affect—I don't even think about, I just do them."

I came back a week later and my friend showed me his completed duck.

"The duck was in the block of wood," I said.

"Yup," he replied, "I knew it would be, but it took a little more time than usual to find it."

To become a master teacher, teaching becomes a part of you. You internalize the role of teacher to the extent that you do many things almost by instinct. You can learn how to think as a teacher, but it is nearly impossible to teach you to think this way. This may sound like a contradiction but it is not. Thinking as a teacher includes a bundle of abilities, attitudes, knowledge, points of view, and ideas all interacting with each other, interacting with you as a person, and coming into play when you teach. When you are thinking as a teacher, you do certain things in certain ways. You may not be fully conscious of why you are doing them—you just know from deep inside that these are the right things to do in this situation.

TEACHING STYLE

You become a master teacher of adults by keeping up-to-date in your content area, by better organizing the materials you use in your teaching, by sharpening your use of teaching tools, by improving participant feedback approaches, and by devising better time management skills both in the planning of teaching activities and in carrying them out. But even with improvement in all these areas, becoming a master teacher requires more.

This additional attribute is thinking as a teacher, and one important dimension of it is *teaching style*.

Your teaching style is the sum of everything you do as a teacher—how you use your hands and your voice, how you interact with learners, and how you organize materials. Imbedded within your style is a philosophy about yourself and what you are doing, about learners and your content, indeed about the world and how you see it.

A teaching style is not something you go looking for and then copy. Every teacher has one. You have a teaching style, and it is distinctive for you. No other teacher works in the same way you do, even with the same materials and the same learners.

Master teachers constantly improve their teaching styles and search for better ways of relating to learners. They consider the widely different learning style preferences, the needs of diverse cultural groups, and the challenges of ever increasing knowledge and often limited time for learning. Master teachers also reflect on ethical questions, realizing that some teaching styles are more ethically appropriate than others. For example, teachers who degrade learners, make them appear foolish in front of their peers, or put them in dependent roles have clearly unethical styles.

FINDING YOUR TEACHING STYLE

On a sheet of paper or in your teaching journal, draw a picture of yourself working as a teacher. It need not be a fancy artistic creation. Stick figures are fine. This exercise produces an interesting array of results. Commonly, the pictures fall into categories which I call teacher metaphors (Postman and Weingartner, 1969, p. 82). Where do you fit?

- *Lamplighters*. They attempt to illuminate the minds of their learners.

- *Gardeners*. Their goal is to cultivate the mind by nourishing, enhancing the climate, removing the weeds and other impediments, and then standing back and allowing growth to occur.

- *Muscle builders*. They exercise and strengthen flabby minds so learners can face the heavyweight learning tasks of the future.

- *Bucket fillers*. They pour information into empty containers with the assumption that a filled bucket is a good bucket. In other words, a head filled with information makes an educated person.

- *Challengers*. They question learners' assumptions, helping them see subject matter in fresh ways and develop critical thinking skills.

- *Travel guides*. They assist people along the path of learning.

- *Factory supervisors*. They supervise the learning process, making certain that sufficient inputs are present and that the outputs are consistent with the inputs.

- *Artists*. For them teaching has no prescriptions and the ends are not clear at the beginning of the process. The entire activity is an aesthetic experience.

- *Applied scientists*. They apply research findings to teaching problems and see scientific research as the basis for teaching.

- *Craftspeople*. They use various teaching skills and are able to analyze teaching situations, apply scientific findings when applicable, and incorporate an artistic dimension into teaching.

Problems are associated with some of these metaphors. For example, the gardener metaphor or some version of it has long been a standard in teaching. Give people the resources and information they need, provide a congenial environment, and learning will proceed nicely. That's true for some, but not for all. Some people benefit greatly when the teacher challenges them by raising questions and inquiring about the assumptions of what they are learning. Learners in challenging situations often emerge as "empowered learners," who can go out on their own and continue to think critically.

Most adults will not put up with the muscle builder approach. People want practical learning that is either immediately useful, soon will be, or has some direct value to them. Learning in and of itself simply does not appeal to many adults.

Unfortunately, the bucket fillers are quite prevalent. The assumption of this teaching approach is: The more information you have, the better educated you will be. Many people these days, myself included, believe that excessive information is itself a problem for many people. By providing increasing quantities of information we may be contributing to the learner's problem rather than helping solve problems.

The factory supervisor metaphor has gained considerable credence during the last decade or so. To be more competitive, businesses have streamlined their production and marketing and expedited their research and development activities. It seems logical that these firms would apply principles of efficiency and expediency to teaching their employees. But as mentioned in Chapter 1, many firms are looking for workers who not only have the necessary job skills but also know how to think creatively and critically.

Look again at the picture of yourself as teacher. Does it fit within one of these categories? If not, how is it different? If it does fit, are you comfortable with your metaphor or do you want to make some changes?

In my judgment, master teachers are challengers, travel guides, gardeners, craftspeople, or some combination of these.

DEVELOPING A VISION

Besides recognizing and developing a teaching style, master teachers have a vision. As a master teacher you are aware of a larger purpose for what you do, similar to the bricklayer who was building a cathedral rather than merely laying bricks. You have aims that transcend the immediate class or workshop that is today's responsibility. You know the importance of helping adults learn something today, but you also are aware of larger goals—the betterment of human lives, the empowerment of people, and a changed, more responsive society.

Your vision needs defining. It becomes your point of light and gives you direction during good and bad times. A vision is built on a solid set of beliefs and understanding about adults as learners and about the teaching process—the subjects of the next two chapters.

CHAPTER 6

Developing a Basis for Teaching

A group of my graduate students, all teachers of adults, came to me one day with a request. They said, "You're giving us all this information about teaching, program planning, and evaluation, but we're concerned about more basic questions."

What did they mean?

"Well," their spokesperson said, "We want to look at some basics. We want to examine some of our basic beliefs about teaching and learning, about adult learners, and about the topics we are studying in our courses. We also want to examine questions we have about our jobs as teachers of adults."

So we began meeting in an informal seminar to discuss these questions. We chose the label "working philosophy" to describe the outcome of what we were doing. We liked the idea that a working philosophy was indeed "working"; that you never finished it, but were constantly improving and developing it. Thus a working philosophy was really a process for examining what you believe rather than something you went looking for, found, and kept the rest of your life. It could be, and likely should be, changed from time to time, as you grow and develop, as societal conditions change, and as your learners change.

The more I thought about it, and the more teachers of adults I helped to develop working philosophies, the more convinced I am that having a working philosophy is essential for becoming a master teacher. Here's how you develop one.

A WORKING PHILOSOPHY

The framework for a working philosophy contains four elements:

1. Your beliefs about adults as learners
2. Your beliefs about aims

27

3. Your beliefs about subject matter
4. Your beliefs about teaching and about learning

The process includes (1) examining what you now know and believe about each of these elements, (2) searching for alternative beliefs, and (3) deciding on a working set of beliefs (See Apps, 1985, for a more comprehensive description).

BELIEFS ABOUT ADULTS AS LEARNERS

Take out your journal and jot down answers to this question: Why do you believe adults want to learn? Describe them as learners, in any way you can.

Some teachers find it useful to reflect on the nature of human nature as a way of understanding their personal beliefs about adults. Some argue that human nature is basically good, some say it's bad, some say it's neutral, and some don't want to talk about human nature.

Teachers often find it useful to reflect on the relationship of adult learners to the context in which they find themselves, their families, and their communities. Some go further and explore the relationships of human beings to the natural environment, pointing out that all life on the planet is related.

But write what matters to you. Write your personal beliefs, not what you think you should believe. A working philosophy is an extremely personal thing; it must be yours.

Once you have written your list, you may want to read Chapter 7, Understanding Adult Learners. Are there now items you would add to your list or items you might drop or change?

BELIEFS ABOUT AIMS

Once again, turn to your teaching journal. This time make a list of your aims for teaching, what you hope to accomplish when you teach. Don't read ahead. Sit back, think for a minute, and write your personal thoughts. Don't be influenced by what you believe someone else says your aims should be. For the moment, don't even worry about your organization or institution's aims. Concentrate on what you believe.

Now look at your list. Do you see your primary aim as being a transmitter of information? In the extreme, I've seen teachers describe themselves as information machines that gather, store, and then parcel out facts to eager learners. Of course providing information will by definition always be a role teachers perform. But is this the sole purpose for being a teacher, or even the most important purpose?

Do you aim to do what the adults in your classes want you to do, always? Of course you want to teach those things your learners expect you to teach. If you don't you'll hear about it, or your supervisor will hear about it and then you'll hear about it. But let me make an important point. Your participants often don't know fully what it is they really want to learn. I'm not suggesting that you know better what people need to know than they do. But you have an obligation, in many situations, to take learners beyond where they are now in their recognition of what they want to learn.

For example, suppose a couple of participants come to a class in word processing interested in learning a software program that is old, clumsy, and difficult to learn—perhaps one of the very early word processing programs. As the teacher, I am familiar with two or three programs that are far superior to the one these participants want to learn. I believe I have an obligation to introduce them to the superior programs. In some instances, participants may not want to learn what I am teaching and I don't think what they want to learn is appropriate. In these situations, I suggest they find another teacher who is willing to teach them what they want to learn or that they reconsider their learning needs.

At a deeper, more complicated level, in many courses the teacher has an obligation to help learners examine positions that they hold about certain things. I believe I have an obligation not only to provide information directly or through reference material, but also to help people to examine this information critically from their own personal perspectives.

For instance, in a class about slavery in certain southern states before 1860, it would be easy to present "the facts" about slavery. But these "facts," as is true of all historical writing, depend on the perspective of the author. So, I would provide several references with multiple perspectives on this topic. Then, through questioning and other teaching techniques, I would begin examining how the participants in the class relate to these different perspectives—how they, as individuals, see the phenomenon of slavery in this country. Such questioning will serve to move learners in my class beyond where they are now, not only in their understanding of several perspectives about slavery, but also about their own beliefs on this issue.

Now, clearly, many of the participants enrolled in the class may have come for the sole reason of gaining more information about slavery. They may not be interested in comparing perspectives—I hope I can convince them that there is no one "correct" perspective and that comparison is vital. I hope that most of them will see the value of examining their own personal perspectives about slavery. Some may choose not to do this, and that is of course their right. But I believe, for a course like this one, I have an obligation to go beyond the mere presentation of information.

Another set of aims that is important for teachers of adults to consider relates to the process of learning. You've probably heard the slogan, "Helping people learn how to learn" as an aim for teaching adults. Helping people to become comfortable with multiple perspectives on issues, to find resources, to concentrate on one topic over an extended time, and to polish their listening, writing, and speaking skills—all are included in learning how to learn.

In addition to assisting people to learn how to learn, I also believe I have an obligation to help people become careful selectors of "what" to learn. The situation in the word processing class is an example of what I mean.

Unlearning is another element in the process of learning. One of the greatest enemies of learning is other learning. Our heads are crammed with obsolete ideas, inappropriate attitudes, and erroneous information. We often aren't aware of what we know that is accurate and up-to-date and what is inaccurate and hopelessly dated. Helping people unlearn is one important aim for our teaching—as painful as the process can be for many people.

At a more philosophical level, is it the primary aim of our teaching to assist individuals to improve themselves; and is it also an appropriate aim to focus directly on societal improvement? In the United States, adult learning has historically focused on benefitting the individual. The argument goes, as individuals learn, grow, and develop, the society, made up of these individuals, will also grow and develop.

Others have pointed out, though, that certain societal problems must be solved by a more direct route, rather than waiting for the sum of all the individual learning—which may or may not eventually address the problem.

Civil rights is a good example. Since the Civil War, schools and education generally said that they aimed to improve relations among the races and make blacks and whites more equal in society. It didn't happen. It took the Civil Rights legislation of the sixties to begin making changes. A massive educational effort, with political activism, demonstrations, and considerable turmoil finally led to the passage of this legislation. The country couldn't wait for individuals to make changes. What was called for was a collective educational effort that led to legislative action.

Of course the process, as well as the outcome, was controversial and continues to be to this day. The question about aims remains—should teachers of adults focus on collective problems, as well as help individuals solve personal problems and meet individual wants?

Master teachers are concerned with a wide sweep of aims. You are never content merely to transmit information to others. In fact, by focusing on information transmission you may, in some instances, inhibit participants' learning rather than enhancing it.

BELIEFS ABOUT SUBJECT MATTER

"Why examine this area?" you ask, adding, "I have subject matter to teach, that's why I was hired, and that's what I do." True. But the question is a bit more complicated, particularly when you think about the subject matter you are teaching in reference to what you believe about adult learners and aims.

Let's examine the very nature of subject matter. It's a human invention. Somebody somewhere talked about or likely wrote about what you are teaching. Subject matter doesn't just happen.

Let's say you teach nature appreciation. You and your class are hiking around a pond in a deep woods shortly after the winter snows have melted. You point out a deer trail pounded into the brown dead grass. You ask the group to remain quiet while a wild turkey gobbles in the distance, and then you hear the drumming of a ruffed grouse far off in the woods. All of what is happening—what you are seeing and hearing and feeling and smelling and perhaps even tasting—is subject matter. It is there, and it is real.

Someone sometime put labels on what you and your group observed. A ruffed grouse and a wild turkey were merely living creatures until someone labeled them and categorized them. Everything we call subject matter, from the readily observable birds and animals in nature to the highly abstract ideas of the political scientist or sociologist, is a human invention.

Categorizing subject matter can influence our view of reality of that subject matter. For instance, believing that all subject matter fits neatly into some labeled category such as psychology or sociology may blind us from even seeing subject matter that doesn't neatly fit within such a category or that overlaps with several categories. At times, a creative cross-disciplinary or even extra-disciplinary approach is what is called for.

Too often, we as teachers dispense subject matter, seldom questioning the accuracy of the labels that are used to describe events, occurrences, thoughts, and ideas. True, it makes little sense to debate whether we should call a ruffed grouse a partridge, as long as we are clear about it and everyone understands what we are discussing. But it does make sense, to me at least, to question whether everyone has a midlife crisis as many developmental psychologists suggest, or that high interest rates always mean a decline in the stock market, or that people over sixty have trouble learning numbers.

Master teachers help learners become critical thinkers. You help them raise questions about subject matter and its categories and labels, without accepting everything as a given.

Adult learners possess considerable accumulated information and knowledge. They have learned on the job, through travel, and through the process of living. As a teacher of adults you know that life experience sets older learners apart from younger learners, but you may have difficulty recognizing that this accumulated life experience is also subject matter for the sessions you are teaching. Another difficulty you may face, once you realize that the life experience represented in any group of adult learners is a valuable resource, is how to tap it. The problem is twofold: (1) how to get this subject matter out on the table and accessible to all, and (2) here's the real challenge—how to help the group sort out what is relevant to the session and what is not.

A politician was speaking to a group of farmers. After the speech went on for a half hour or so, one old white-bearded farmer in the back row nudged his neighbor and whispered, "What's he talking about?"

His neighbor replied, "He doesn't say."

As those of you with more experience know, some participants, once they begin, keep on talking and talking. I fear some of them keep on talking, hoping they will think of something to say.

Those who talk too much, participants who insist on sharing the irrelevant—these are the challenges that go with a group sharing its subject matter. Still, when you examine the great benefits that can come from this sharing, the problems become quite insignificant.

BELIEFS ABOUT TEACHING AND LEARNING

Once again take out your teaching journal. At the top of a page write the words, "When I teach I:" Then write whatever comes to mind to complete that sentence. Don't worry about complete sentences; write words, ideas, or phrases. Close this book and take five minutes to complete your list.

My guess is you had little trouble writing down words. I have used this exercise in many workshops and classes. Here are examples of what other teachers have written. When I teach I:

- Have fun

- Provide information

- Help people make sense out of information they already have

- Help people unlearn

- Encourage the nonparticipants; hold back those who may talk too much

- Make people think

- Try to give people what they want

- Use humor

- Make sure participants get their money's worth

- Use participant's examples

- Involve learners in the process

- Care about what I am doing

- Express a passion for my subject and my teaching

- Plan carefully, but stay open to change

- Pay attention to learners, and make slight adjustments in what I do and how I do it based on learner reactions

- Put my entire self into my work

Are any of these phrases your phrases? My guess is that you wrote many of the same ideas, perhaps using slightly different words. What you wrote is a window to what you believe about teaching and about learning. Which of the above statements would a master teacher write? Most, if not all of them. In one way or another, all of these dimensions of teaching appear in this book.

What do you believe about learning? How would you describe it? Here's how I see learning. I developed these beliefs from many years of teaching adults in a variety of settings, ranging from cold hay sheds where farmers learned about up-to-date nutrition requirements of sheep to the shadows of huge old pine trees in northern Wisconsin where creative writing classes met. The second source for my beliefs comes from the considerable research and writing about adult development, learning, motivation, and instructional strategies (see References).

I am convinced that adults do not learn in an ordered and sequential way. The process is turbulent with peaks, valleys, and plateaus, fits and starts, moving forward and sliding back. I am aware that many learners are frustrated when they are attending a workshop or enrolled in a class and they are not learning all the time. As I teacher I was frustrated about this too, but it is a perfectly normal thing. All of us need downtime to allow our extremely elaborate brains to work on the new ideas, new information, new skills, or whatever it is we are learning. It takes time. On the surface we may feel we are not learning, but we are. Indeed, this downtime is likely the most important time in the learning process.

Some people learn best by looking at the whole picture first and then examining the pieces. Others want to start with the pieces, add them together, and create a whole.

People have other preferences. Some like to learn in groups and enjoy the interchange, the motivation, and the social dimension of learning. Others prefer to learn by themselves, off in the corner, off in the library, or in the woods, it doesn't matter where as long as other people aren't there to bother them.

Some people prefer learning when they are talked to—that is, they enjoy a well-developed, carefully presented lecture. Still others prefer to learn visually; they enjoy films, video tapes, and other visual materials. Learning from words is often more difficult for them, particularly if no visual materials are included. Some prefer to learn by doing, a hands-on approach. If they can actually do something, whether it's practice on a computer or learn about group dynamics by practicing with a group, they prefer it.

As you reflect on various approaches to learning and your own preferences, it may be useful to examine some descriptions of learning.

Adult learning is:

- accumulation of information

- change in behavior

- improved performance or proficiency

- change in knowledge, attitudes, and skills

- a new sense of meaning

- cognitive restructuring

- personal transformation

How you see adult learning certainly influences how you teach. No one of these ideas about learning is necessarily the "right" one. Most teachers in particular situations will follow one or more of these descriptions.

Master teachers work at developing a basis for their teaching—a working philosophy. The task is never completed, but continues throughout their careers.

CHAPTER 7

Understanding Adult Learners

When I teach workshops and courses on understanding adult learners, I usually start by asking people to think about themselves as learners.

EXERCISE—DRAWING YOU AS A LEARNER

So, take out a blank sheet of paper, or turn to a blank page in your teaching journal and draw a picture of yourself as a learner. If you're stuck and don't know where to start, here are some hints.

When I ask teachers to draw pictures of themselves as learners, some draw trees—they see the roots going down and the branches spreading widely as they continue to learn. Others draw pictures of trains on tracks winding toward unknown horizons. Still others sketch pictures of mountains and plains. They depict themselves struggling up steep mountain trails, and other times jogging across flat plains with the warm sun shining on their backs, and multicolored wild flowers lining the path.

I think you get the idea. Now close this book, take a deep breath, relax, and begin drawing. Let your imagination and your inner self guide you. Don't worry if your work is not an artistic creation. Just draw a picture of yourself as a learner.

With your picture in front of you, let's try to make some sense out of what you have drawn. In addition to the examples I mentioned above, some teachers draw a flower or a garden of flowers to picture themselves as learners. They see themselves growing and developing over time. New information and warm, pleasant teaching environments assist the growth process.

Occasionally, someone will draw a machine or a variation of a machine. They compare themselves as learners to a computer or some other sophisticated machine that needs a little adjusting from time to time, maybe some reprogramming, but generally the machine can hum along with little assistance.

Still others draw a picture that is a variation of the traveler on a journey. Your picture may illustrate obstacles to overcome—stones in the road or slippery stretches or gullies where rains have washed away the roadway and the path is missing. It may show a crossroads and your indecision as to which road to take. Whatever your theme, look at yourself as a learner. It may assist you in understanding all adult learners.

What are your reasons for learning? Some participants learn for job-related reasons—to do a job better, to find a new job, or to prepare themselves for a promotion where they work. Others learn because they simply want to know more about something or want a new perspective about an event that is occurring in the world. Others enjoy studying history or literature or music or a host of other topics for the sheer joy of it. Sometimes learners want to improve or develop some personal skill, for example, public speaking, writing, dealing with conflict, or operating a personal computer. Almost all of us, from time to time, set out to improve our skills—and this of course involves learning.

You may find that your learning is a secondary outcome to something else you are working on. For instance, you may be involved in a committee to improve your local school. As the committee discusses options for action, you, of necessity, are learning much. You learn about groups and how they function, and you learn about the school's problems from several perspectives. You find out how schools in other parts of the country attempt to solve similar problems.

Most of us learn for a variety of reasons. At any one time we may learn for vocational reasons, for personal growth, or for the sheer joy of learning. And, as I explained with the school committee example, we learn much by working on projects that have goals beyond our personal learning.

We also learn in our day-to-day living without even being aware of it. When we travel we learn. When we begin working with a new co-worker we learn. When we attend a movie, or a play, or a musical concert we learn. We often aren't so aware of this because we didn't set out with learning in mind when we bought the tickets, for instance. But learn we do, almost all the time.

Our learning as adults can be deliberate. That is, we may set out to do it, with a goal in mind. But much more of our learning is non-deliberate. Non-deliberate learning is as important and sometimes more important than that which we learn from our deliberate learning efforts.

Drawing a picture of yourself as a learner is one way to find out how you see other learners, for your picture is in many ways the mirror of what you believe. Many of your characteristics as an adult learner will be similar to those whom you teach. But be careful. There is also considerable diversity among learners. Just because you learn in a particular way doesn't mean everyone learns in a similar manner. In fact, a common error made by novice teachers, and some longtime teachers as well, is to assume that everyone learns as we do.

Let's a look for a moment at the learner from your perspective as a teacher. Turn back to the picture you drew in Chapter 5 of yourself as teacher.

What does your teacher picture say about how you see adults as learners? Do you see adults in your class or workshop as mostly passive, waiting for you to provide them with information or to show them how to do something? Do you see them as people who depend on you as the teacher to help them understand something or learn a new skill? Or, do you see them as active participants, challenging and raising questions and moving toward less dependence on you and more dependence on themselves as learners?

CHARACTERISTICS OF ADULT LEARNERS

In the past, researchers gave almost no attention to characteristics of adults as learners; the emphasis was on children and youth. Fortunately research describing adults as learners is now easily available (see References). Here is a brief description of some of that literature which those in my classes and workshops have found useful in their work.

Learner's History

An adult's personal history can affect greatly what and how that individual learns. Neil Postman and Charles Weingartner (1969, p. 90), authors and critics of education, discuss early perception studies and conclude that how people perceive comes from within them—their previous experiences, their childhoods, and their formal schooling. What these studies say is this—when we present information to a group of, for example, fifteen people, there is a good chance that what we say can be perceived fifteen different ways. As teachers, we can't assume that how we perceive something is how everyone else will perceive it. Sometimes the differences are subtle and not immediately evident. We may believe that everyone understands something in the same way and later learn this is not the case.

Some people also argue there is no "right way" for perceiving something and that we should expect, indeed encourage, multiple perceptions. This leads us to a philosophical discussion of where do we draw the line— are some people's perceptions simply wrong and do we have some obligation to help them see that wrongness through a critical examination?

Not only does personal history influence perception, it also influences what people do with new information—how they organize it, what they keep and what they discard, and how they relate new information to previous information that they perceive as similar.

Our personal histories form the basis for our world views—the set of beliefs we hold that guide our day-to-day activities. Our world view includes the assumptions we hold about such things as politics, the nature of human nature, our definition of progress, the place for technology in society, and so on. Thus personal histories have great influence on nearly all aspects of our lives. As teachers we must take into account personal histories when we teach—both ours and those of the participants in our classes and workshops.

Preferred Learning Style

Research studies tell us that people learn in different ways, and they prefer different learning styles. Robert Smith (1982), author of *Learning How To Learn*, defines learning style as "the individual's characteristic ways of processing information, feeling, and behaving in learning situations" (p. 24).

Some of the dimensions of learning style preferences include desire for: "hands on" learning, listening, problem solving, visual materials, reading, starting with the "big picture," starting with pieces of information to build the big picture, learning by one's self, learning with others, learning in a step-by-step fashion, and learning intuitively. Many people prefer a combination of several learning approaches—for instance, some like to read, try out by themselves what they are learning, and discuss their learning with others.

Researchers have developed a variety of learning style inventories to help learners and teachers understand more about individual preferences. These include Kolb's Learning Style Inventory, the Canfield Learning Styles Inventory, Witkin's Embedded Figures Test, the Gregorc approach, and Myers-Briggs Type Indicator.

Though these inventories can be helpful, learning style preference is far too complicated for measuring with a simple test. At this stage in our knowledge of learning style preferences, about the best we can do is provide variety in our teaching approaches, hoping to accommodate as wide a diversity of learning style preferences as possible. Chapter 11 contains detailed ideas about relating teaching approaches to learning styles.

One other interesting point—some people prefer a particular learning style because that is the only way in which they have experienced learning. They may have spent a lifetime having teachers lecture to them, and thus they say they prefer lecturing. Sometimes, by encouraging them to try other learning strategies, they discover that they really prefer quite a different approach.

Social Setting for Adult Learners

Because of their busy lives which usually include family, work, and social responsibilities, adult learners prefer some control over the place, pace, and time they learn. Work and personal responsibilities often prevent their traveling long distances to learning sites. Thus learning opportunities in the workplace or in the community have become popular.

Many adults, also because of busy schedules, want some say over how fast or how slowly they learn something. And, finally, because of personal scheduling challenges, adult learners want choices for when they learn—evenings, early mornings, weekends, or some other convenient time.

Motivation for Learning

According to Carol Aslanian and Henry Bricknell (1980), researchers with the New York based College Board, the majority of adults participate in learning because of some trigger event in their lives: a divorce, a new job, a lost job, a new baby, loss of a loved one, moving to a new location, retirement, or some similar major event. The idea of a "teachable moment" appears to come into play. Just preceding or immediately after a significant trigger occurs is often the prime time for people to seek learning related to this trigger event.

The majority of adults participate in adult education because of a relationship to vocation. They want to improve on their current job, they seek a promotion, they want a different job, or they must keep up to date to retain their present job. For women who have been out of the job market for several years, participation in education is often seen as a step toward obtaining a job.

Some adults (far fewer than those with vocational interests) seek learning because of a basic interest in a topic or for the pure love of learning. The great success of the Elderhostel program for retired people attests to this for most of the offerings are not of a "practical" nature but are more tuned to such topics as understanding great literature and art, appreciating nature, or enriching travel experiences.

Understanding the nature of the developmental phases adults pass through in their lives also helps us understand motivation for learning. As adults go from one phase to another, they often seek understanding of the new phase in light of the experience and knowledge they gained from the previous phase. The various life span researchers generally focus on three broad types of changes in a person's life: physical change, emotional change, and cognitive change.

Psychological Dimensions

Adult learners are often quite unsure of themselves, particularly when they first enroll in a course that may meet for several times over a period of weeks. Very soon they want to know how they are doing; they expect feedback. This feedback need not come via a formal examination. It could result from a written assignment or a personal comment from the teacher. Honesty and diplomacy are also important. If a learner is not doing well, she or he deserves to know this, but we must present the message in such a way that the person doesn't give up.

As increasing numbers of older adults begin entering our classes and workshops, we must be aware of changes that occur in people as they age. We may need to speak louder and perhaps slower. We must remember to make larger visuals. Although older adults may not learn as quickly as young people, they have a tremendous capacity for learning. Don't confuse speed with ability. Slower learning time doesn't mean reduced ability.

Preference for the Practical

Most adult learners have a practical reason for their learning. They want to learn something that they can apply immediately. *Praxis* is a word often used to identify the process whereby people learn something, try it out in a practical situation, reflect on what happened, refine the learning, try it again, reflect, and so on. Many adults regularly carry out praxis as a natural approach to their learning.

Historically, educators have worked on the assumption that what young people learn now will be useful to them in some indefinite future. For most adults the future is now. That doesn't mean excluding theoretical dimensions of subject matter—but tying the theory to practice, if possible. On the other hand, sizeable numbers of adults want to study topics that do not appear practical—in the sense of immediate application. They want to know more about the arts, about world politics, about history and religion.

Becoming a master teacher requires that you understand adults as learners. As you teach, you will increasingly gain insights about learners. This is both the great challenge of a personal approach to teaching as well as a great joy.

CHAPTER 8

Teaching Tools for Providing Information and Skill Training

The next three chapters present a collection of teaching tools with a brief explanation of how to use each one. The tools are organized according to various teaching purposes: to provide information, skill training, critical thinking, and so on. That's not to suggest that you can't take tools from any of the categories and use them for other purposes. For example, If you want to try a case study approach for presenting information, do it. In addition, many of the teaching tools may be combined in the same class or workshop. See Chapter 11 for suggestions on how to select teaching tools.

I have used these tools in my teaching. Some I developed myself, others are modifications of standard teaching approaches. I would encourage you, as you gain experience teaching, to do the same thing. Try the tools and then modify them to fit your own situation. I encourage you to invent new tools and new teaching approaches that fit you, your learners, and your particular kinds of learning situations.

TOOLS FOR PROVIDING INFORMATION

LECTURE

This is probably the most criticized of all the teaching tools I discuss in this book. Some teachers of adults argue that the lecture should never be used ever. I am certainly not advocating that you do all of your teaching following the lecture method, but there is a place for lectures, particularly short, succinct presentations used in conjunction with other teaching tools. Lecturing continues to be one of the most efficient and effective tools for presenting information. In order to be effective, lectures must be done well.

Tips for Preparing and Delivering Lectures

Lecture no longer than thirty minutes at a time.

Include no more than four or five major points, and be clear about which particular point you are discussing. Summarize main points at the end of the presentation.

Make sure you can be heard.

Enhance the impact of lectures with visuals such as chalkboard, newsprint, overhead projection visuals, slides, and videotape clips.

Use stories (not jokes, although stories may be humorous) to keep interest and help amplify major points.

Keep language as simple and concrete as subject matter allows. The more abstract the ideas, the more stories you need.

Keep eye contact with the group.

Allow learners time to take notes.

Make sure all learners can see visual material you use. Don't stand in front of the chalkboard or screen.

Allow time for audience questions at the end of the lecture.

Provide learners a written handout of major points covered in the lecture, and where they can find additional information on this topic.

Start on time, end on time.

Be enthusiastic; believe what you are saying.

Avoid

Reading from a manuscript. You may put yourself to sleep.

Talking too fast, too slowly, too softly, or in a monotone.

Tugging your ear, shuffling your notes, clearing your throat, saying "and ah" or "you know." Watch yourself on videotape or have a friend or spouse sit in and honestly report your performance quirks.

Believing that lecturing is the one and only way to teach, now and forever.

Believing that lecturing is the ultimate in poor teaching and never should be used when teaching adults.

INTERVIEW

I use the interview occasionally, particularly when I bring a resource person to my class, who is not accustomed to speaking in front of a group. I sit in front of the class with this person and we conduct a discussion based on questions I have prepared. Sometimes I send a copy of the questions to the person ahead of time, but frankly the interview is often more interesting when it is spontaneous and unplanned. I usually ask a few questions, then encourage the class members to ask questions as well. This works well if the group is relatively small (less than thirty members).

Tips for Preparing

Carefully select a resource person who knows the subject you want to explore and at the same time is articulate and forthright with answers.

Meet with the resource person before the class to discuss what you plan to do, giving either a list of questions or examples of questions you plan to ask.

Suggest the person be brief with responses.

Think carefully about the questions that will be asked, and what you want to accomplish with this tool.

Avoid

Asking general questions that result in vague answers.

Having the resource person give a series of short speeches in response to questions.

Sticking tightly to a list of prepared questions. Answers often evoke new questions which add excitement to the process.

FIELD TRIP

For many topics that you teach, a field trip is an excellent tool for providing information. For instance, if you are teaching a course in gardening, a visit to a garden center might be in order. If your course is on modern art, then visiting a art center will likely add to what you present in class. To be effective, field trips require considerable planning.

Tips for Preparing and Carrying Out

Visit the site before the trip, and discuss with the guide what you want the class to see and do.

Pay particular attention to all details such as transportation and meals.

Discuss with participants what they should look for on the trip.

Pay particular attention to any participants with physical disabilities.

Make certain that all participants will be able to see and hear.

After the trip, help the participants analyze what they saw, its meaning, and the relationship of what they learned on the trip to other topics discussed in the course.

Be prepared for the unexpected, and be able to adjust with grace and a sense of humor.

Avoid

Taking a field trip without clear objectives and prior planning.

PRINT MATERIALS

Unfortunately, many teachers tend to take print materials for granted. They may provide a reading list and sometimes even require certain things be read, but they don't consider the difficulty that some participants will have in gaining access to the materials.

Another error that some teachers make is failing to be specific about readings. If you expect people to read something, then you must be specific about what you expect, when you expect it, and then make sure that learners have access to the materials.

I've also learned that some participants want to read beyond the requirements. So I usually provide a bibliography of additional readings for those who want to go further.

When I'm conducting workshops, I try to have copies of supplemental readings in the room, so participants can browse through them during breaks and decide if they want to read further.

Tips for Using Print Materials

In a course where reading is a requirement, provide one textbook, rather than several, or photocopy chapters from several books, magazines, or journals and make them available in a package. Follow copyright laws; your photocopy center has them.

Be clear about what materials you expect learners to read between class or workshop sessions.

Encourage learners to keep a journal where they write responses to what they are reading—questions, comments, and disagreements. Encourage more than merely copying a series of quotations from the readings.

Be prepared to suggest particular readings for participants with specific interests who want to go beyond the requirements.

Make certain that required reading materials are central to the topics you discuss in class and not seen as unrelated or merely "nice to know" information.

Distribute written handout materials during class sessions. Use a three-hole punch, so materials fit in notebooks. keep them.

Avoid

Expecting more reading than adult learners with work, family and other responsibilities can handle.

Expecting no reading, particularly when many adult learners look forward to enhancing what they are learning in class.

Giving no direction to learners about how to organize their reading.

Failing to recognize the great diversity in the amount of reading participants will do. Some will want to go well beyond what you suggest.

RESULT DEMONSTRATION

When I worked as a county extension agent for University of Wisconsin-Extension, I often used result demonstrations as a way to show learners exactly how something I was teaching might be applied. In those days I was teaching agricultural topics including teaching farmers about grain varieties they might consider planting. I would ask two or three farmers in different locations to grow several different grain varieties. Then, several times during the summer, I would conduct meetings at the demonstration farms and we would inspect the varieties and discuss their growth characteristics.

Such topics as office management procedures could be taught following this approach. Select one or more offices where the manager is willing to introduce the ideas you are teaching. Then the class could visit this office occasionally, over a period of time, to see how the procedures worked, what problems were encountered, how employees reacted and the like.

Tips for Using

Carefully select the cooperators. They must be people willing to follow directions carefully and to follow through with the demonstration.

Be clear about the purposes for the result demonstration. That is, know what results you want to demonstrate.

Work out an agreement with the cooperator concerning the costs of the demonstration.

As the teacher, visit the demonstration site regularly, taking pictures, recording information about progress, and supervising the cooperator to make sure directions are followed.

Select logical times for group visits. Invite those whom you believe would be interested in the demonstration.

Capture as much information as possible about the demonstration via video tape, audio tape and print. You can use this in other classes, workshops, and conferences.

Avoid

Selecting a demonstration and a demonstrator and then not taking the time to carefully supervise the operation.

Attempting a result demonstration for subject matter unsuited to this approach.

TOOLS FOR SKILL TRAINING

INTERACTIVE COMPUTERS

Increasingly, computers have become a part of skill training. They can be a powerful tool both to help the teacher and to enhance participant learning. They don't replace the teacher. People who are learning by interacting with a cold, impersonal machine need the teacher's presence as much or more than those who attend more traditional classes.

In my experience with interactive computers, information is presented on a screen, either in printed format or through graphic or audio medium, or some combination of these forms. The learners, each working individually on a computer, answer questions or solve problems and receive immediate feedback. Learners can interact individually with the instructional material, proceeding at their own pace.

Learners often run into snags. The equipment doesn't work properly, or they don't understand what the computer program is trying to tell them. The whole process is just too impersonal for many people. Here's where you can help by providing assurance, showing people how to operate the equipment, and being available to answer any questions.

Tips for Using

Make certain learners know how to operate the computers.

Be available to help learners who have difficulty with the computer's instructions.

Be aware that not all participants learn equally well with interactive computer programs.

Realize that some learners will take much longer than others to master the same skill. Allow them time to repeat the program until they have mastered the skill.

Avoid

Closely observing participants while they work.

Encouraging individual learners to cover the skill training in unison, as if they were a group.

Making negative comments to participants who take longer to learn a skill.

SKILL DEMONSTRATION

Some years ago I taught basic photography classes to people who had recently purchased 35mm cameras. Since this was before the advent of automatic cameras, I often demonstrated how to load film, adjust the shutter speed, and so on.

For many kinds of skills, learners gain much by watching the teacher perform the skill. I usually combined a skill demonstration with a short lecture about what I was doing and why, followed by letting the participants try the skill (see Hands-on With Supervision below).

Tips for Using

Be well prepared, which means practicing before class.

Have an example of a finished product to show, if there is one.

Have all needed materials out and ready to use.

Make certain that all participants can see and hear what you are doing.

Be deliberate, emphasizing each step of what you are demonstrating.

Repeat those elements of the process that are most difficult.

Allow for questions. For some demonstrations, questions may be answered during the process; for others, questions are best held until the end.

When feasible, provide a written copy of the steps that have been demonstrated, or give out a written guide at the beginning of the demonstration so participants can follow along. Some learners will take notes on the handout as you speak.

Avoid

Moving too quickly.

Assuming participants may be familiar with some of the steps and therefore not spending enough time.

Dismissing some questions as inappropriate, which discourages other participants from asking questions.

Assuming a superior attitude about your skills which may discourage learners from trying to master the skill.

HANDS-ON WITH SUPERVISION

As I mentioned above, when you are teaching skills you will generally combine some lecturing and a skills demonstration with providing time for participants to practice the skill.

Tips for Using

Provide times when learners can come to you for additional help, if they want it.

Be patient with learners' errors.

If the skill involves safety (use of woodworking equipment, for instance), make certain safety cautions are clear to everyone.

Be willing to demonstrate again whatever steps a learner is having difficulty with.

Be particularly patient with participants learning hand skills when they are left-handed and you are right-handed, or vice versa.

Allow time for learners to practice the skill unobserved. Some learners become nervous when you look over their shoulder.

Encourage participants to help each other.

Avoid

Expecting that everyone will grasp the idea on the first attempt.

Making discouraging comments.

Embarrassing learners in front of their peers.

Losing your patience with learners who seem to have no grasp of the skill.

INTERNSHIP

For longer term training periods, when you are working with a group of learners who are interested in learning clusters of skills, the internship can be extremely valuable. I use internships often with graduate students who are interested in making a career change and have little or no practical experience in their desired career. You can devise many types of internships, depending on the time available and the interest of the learners. For the internship to work well, however, the participant (intern) must spend enough time actually working in the new job not only to learn how to do it, but to learn something about the relationships with other people and the organization itself.

For instance, recently several of my graduate students have wanted to become trainers. I helped them line up internships with firms in our area that have training departments. In almost every instance, these students said this was one of the best parts of their graduate program.

Interns usually serve from two or three weeks to a year. After some observation time, the intern usually has the opportunity to perform the tasks expected of someone working in the particular setting.

Tips for Planning and Conducting Internships

With the intern and the on-site supervisor, plan carefully what the intern is expected to learn.

Plan to have periodic meetings with the on-site supervisor and the intern to discuss progress and problems.

Design the learning plan to include progression from observation to direct involvement in a series of tasks representative of the work setting.

Orient the intern to the internship setting—what to expect, what the work rules are, and so on. A visit to the internship setting prior to the assignment may help to clarify many of these questions.

If several interns are working on internships, hold periodic seminars for interns to share their experiences with each other. See Chapter 9 for a discussion of seminars.

Encourage interns to keep daily journals of what they did, what they learned, and the meaning of it all.

Ask interns, upon completion of an internship, to write a report that summarizes what they learned from the experience, what questions the experience raised, and what further learning was suggested.

Avoid

Placing an intern in a setting where there is inadequate on-site supervision.

Placing an intern in a setting where the intern is expected to complete the same tasks throughout the entire internship without the opportunity to experience a variety of tasks or more complicated tasks.

Placing an intern without sufficient preparation on what to expect.

CASE STUDY

When it is difficult to do the real thing, because of time, money, or other reasons, a case study can be a reasonable alternative. You present a problem situation to a small group for them to analyze and solve. The case study approach usually emphasizes a process for analysis, rather than for teaching specific information.

Tips for Using

Obtain existing case studies. For instance, business schools often use case studies for teaching business principles.

Develop your own case study from real life situations. Disguise the names and descriptions of people and places to avoid embarrassment and possible legal problems. Occasionally stories in newspapers or magazines can be developed into case studies.

In developing case studies, concentrate on presenting facts. Try to make the situation as real as possible with conversations between people, descriptions of events, and so on. The entire case study can be a creation with no direct tie to a real situation, but it must appear realistic.

Select or create case studies that fit the backgrounds and experience of participants as well as fit the learning objectives.

Explain to the group that careful analysis must precede the selection of solutions.

Provide specific questions at the end of the case to direct the group members. For example, for cases involving interpersonal problems, questions might be: What would you do? Why? With whom? How would you do it? When?

Give participants a specific time for working on the case study. Test your case ahead of time so you know how long learners will take to analyze and reach solutions.

Ask each group to present to the total group its analysis and solution to the case situation.

Lead a group discussion about the problem solving process, the difficulties groups experienced with the case study, and what they gained from the activity.

Avoid

Having long complex case studies (unless you want to focus an entire learning experience, over time, on such an analysis).

Moving learners into a case study exercise without explaining the importance of the problem solving process with particular attention to careful analysis.

Leaving the impression there is only one right answer to a case.

CHAPTER 9

Teaching Tools for Developing In-Depth Understanding

This chapter will present several teaching tools I have found particularly useful for helping participants develop a deeper understanding and wider perspective about what they are learning. These tools go well beyond merely helping adults gain new information or learn new skills. They can help adults experience as well as learn critical thinking skills. See Chapter 12 for more information about teaching critical thinking.

TOOLS FOR DEVELOPING IN-DEPTH UNDERSTANDING

FORUM

I use this teaching approach when I bring a resource person to my class or workshop, and I want the participants to have an opportunity to interact with the person.

The forum follows the resource person's speech. I plan for fifteen minutes to an hour of open discussion. I encourage participants to offer their opinions on the topic, to raise and discuss issues, and to challenge comments the resource person makes, as well as to question each other's comments. As teacher, I moderate the discussion.

Tips for Planning and Conducting

Be clear about what you want to accomplish with the forum.

Make certain that the resource person has agreed to participate and understands how it works.

Explain to the class what a forum is and how you plan to use it.

Work at balancing contributions from as many class members as possible. This may mean politely calling a halt to an extended comment.

Make sure everyone can hear.

Be prepared to jump in with appropriate questions or comments if the discussion lags.

Avoid

Allowing a few participants to monopolize the time.

Allowing the resource person to give additional short speeches.

QUIET MEETING

This is an excellent tool for five to twenty people who know each other quite well. The key to success is not allowing people to engage in a discussion. Participants sit quietly in a circle and reflect, sharing an idea from time to time, but not dwelling on it or encouraging comment from others.

The group focuses on a topic or question written on the chalkboard or flip chart. Someone in the circle may share a personal experience related to the topic, express a feeling, or add information. The other participants do not react to the person's comments. They are of course free to make their own comments when they wish to. The power of the quiet circle is in the moments of silence when people are thinking and feeling and not talking or listening. When I lead a quiet circle, I ask the participants to "savor the silence." Use this tool when the group believes it can benefit from reflection and contemplation.

Tips for Planning and Conducting

Stress that accepting quiet time as useful for learning is a necessary prerequisite.

Explain the rules.

Participate by making limited contributions.

Be prepared to react to participants who cannot bear long periods of silence. You may need to talk with them privately about their concerns, and about what can be gained from quiet contemplation.

Avoid

Allowing the quiet meeting to degenerate into a group discussion.

Having group members respond to comments others make.

Locating the meeting in a place with distracting noises.

DIAD AND TRIAD

If the group is larger than forty-five or fifty, this tool gets people talking and reacting to what the speaker has said.

After a lecture, ask the group to break into two's or three's and meet for up to five minutes to discuss an assigned question or to identify questions from the presentation. A reporter from each diad or triad summarizes its discussion for the total group. If time is a problem, representative reports can be given from various sections of the room. This technique can be used in a lecture hall with fixed seats.

Tips for Using

Be clear about what you want the diads and triads to do.

Specify the time allotted for the discussion and let the groups know when they have two minutes left.

Circulate among the groups to help answer questions.

Ask each diad or triad to select its own recorder/reporter.

Give instructions on how to form the groups: "Turn to the person next to you," "Turn to the person seated behind you," "Form a group with the two other people at your table."

During the reporting phase, summarize what the groups have said and write comments on a chalkboard or newsprint.

Avoid

Giving vague instructions such as "Discuss the lecture for five minutes."

Letting groups meet beyond the assigned time.

Comparing one group's responses with another, as if one group developed correct answers and others were wrong.

BUZZ GROUP

This is a longer and larger version of the diad and triad technique. Following a lecture or other formal presentation, break the total group into smaller groups of four to six to discuss an assigned question or issue for ten to fifteen minutes. Ask each group to select a recorder who reports results to the total group.

Tips for Using

Have a plan for organizing the groups. Suggest people seated around each table form a group, or people in every other row turn to the people in back of them.

Be clear about what you want the buzz groups to do.

Specify the time allotted for the discussion and let the groups know when they have two minutes left.

Circulate among the groups to help answer questions.

Ask each buzz group to select its own recorder/reporter.

During the reporting phase, summarize what the groups have said and write comments on a chalkboard or newsprint.

Avoid

Giving vague instructions such as "Discuss the lecture for ten minutes."

Letting groups meet beyond the assigned time.

Comparing one group's responses with another, as if one group developed correct answers and others were wrong.

GROUP DISCUSSION

This is a classic teaching tool in adult education. I have used it often as a way of involving people and sharing ideas, and as an approach for encouraging people to interact with me and what I have to offer.

Discussion groups work best when they are no smaller than five or six nor larger than twenty-five or thirty. Participants in a group discussion must have some knowledge of the topic to be discussed, either from assigned readings, previous lectures or other formal presentations, or from personal experience. Participants are generally seated in a circle to facilitate easy contact with each other. Emphasis is on interaction among group members and on sharing of experience and points of view.

Tips for Using

Sit in the circle with the participants.

Use an "ice breaker" exercise so people can become acquainted. See Chapter 10 for suggestions.

Be specific about what the group will discuss.

Limit introductory comments about the topic to fifteen minutes or less.

Keep the discussion directed and on the topic. This often means raising specific questions from time to time with the group, asking people to be more specific if their contributions seem vague, and summarizing whenever you believe the discussion is wandering. Sometimes it helps to write the summary statements on a chalkboard or newsprint to help the group focus its attention.

Bring people into the discussion who are reluctant to speak. ("John, do you have an idea about this question?" "We haven't heard from Mary yet, what do you think about this?")

Politely discourage people who want to dominate the discussion. ("Thank you, Tom, but we really must move on." "An interesting perspective, Jane, does anyone else have a view on this?")

Avoid

Allowing the discussion to drift without direction or purpose.

Using group discussion when the group members do not have sufficient background or information to make a discussion worthwhile.

Embarrassing anyone in the group by making light of a comment or question.

"Forcing" people to participate who wish to be "silent" participants. This does not mean they shouldn't be given an opportunity to participate.

Dominating the group with your own comments, suggestions, directions, and opinions.

SIMULATION GAME

This tool involves participants in situations similar to those which they may face in real life. Games may be paper and pencil activities with a series of problems to be solved, with new information fed into the process as the game progresses, and chance put into the game via card spinners and other devices. Games may also involve computer simulations where participants work the entire game by acting and reacting to information presented on a computer screen.

Tips for Using

Provide participants with background information about the subject matter the game addresses before beginning the game. For some games, you may want to immediately launch into the game, with a discussion of its purpose held until the game is completed.

If it is a team game, select teams carefully so that they are balanced. Avoid placing shy participants on the same team with the most aggressive participants.

Stop the game from time to time to assess progress, problems, and frustrations. Participants may also want to share strategies they are using in working the game.

When developing your own game, make certain it is appropriate for the learners' level of understanding and background information about the topic.

At the completion of the game, spend time discussing what was learned, what difficulties people had, and how particular problems were solved (Adapted from "National Association," 1972, pp. 28–31).

ROLE PLAYING

This is an enjoyable tool to use, and one from which participants usually gain a great deal. Role playing is an excellent way for participants to experience a situation in a safe environment. It works well when study-ing interpersonal relationships, practicing job interviews, exploring com-munity issues, or probing topics where emotions run high and several perspectives are involved.

Tips for Using and What To Avoid

Involve no more than three or four people in a role play with the remainder of the group observing. Additional role plays may involve other members of the group.

Carefully select the role players to avoid the possibility of some persons embarrassing themselves. Oftentimes you will want to select the players before the class meets so they have an chance to think about their roles.

Develop specific roles for each role play member in sufficient detail. For example, if you are role playing a job interview, you might have the interviewer stress asking questions about ability to get along with people. The job candidate is instructed to mention that one of his shortcomings is inability to relate well with others. Do not let role players see each other's specific role assignments. Role players have no script. They must feel their roles and say what they believe the situation demands.

While role players are making final preparations, direct the group to look for specific behaviors, emotional reactions, and underlying forces that emerge in the role playing drama.

Stop the role play when sufficient information has been presented for a discussion. Avoid having the role play continue too long.

Upon completion of the role play, ask the role players how they felt about their roles and what they learned from the experience. Ask the entire group what insights they got from the role play experience.

When discussing the role playing event, monitor the discussion to help ensure the discussion is about the roles played and the meaning of them, rather than about the people who played the roles.

GROUP PROJECT

If you are teaching a class that meets over a period of time, this is an excellent tool to help participants learn together. From two to four participants work together on a project such as tracking down specific information on a topic and presenting it to the class, building something in a woodworking workshop, developing a class presentation on some topic, or a similar task.

Tips for Using

Be sure projects have meaning and are not merely "make work" activities.

Encourage participants to turn in a project proposal. This allows the teacher to provide comments and make suggestions for resources.

Give group members a clear idea of what product is expected of their effort.

Allow participants to select their own projects without domination from the instructor.

Be available for consultation when asked.

Avoid

Supervising the group's activities too closely.

SEMINAR

With this teaching tool, learners are encouraged to explore personal learning projects and then report the results of their efforts to the total seminar group. I use this approach when I am offering a general topic, such as future directions for continuing education agencies. Each seminar participant selects one rather specific idea within that topic and explores it in depth. Not only do participants learn about a given topic, and learn what other participants have found out, but they get practice in self-directed learning.

During the first seminar I usually spend some time discussing ways of finding, organizing, and presenting information on topics. Then, at succeeding sessions, I make some introductory comments, then turn the session over to a participant to make a presentation. I lead a group discussion following the presentation. The seminar works best with groups of five to fifteen. Often the seminar participants provide both a written as well as an oral presentation to the group.

Tips for Using

Ensure that seminar topics chosen by participants are consistent with knowledge and ability of the teacher.

Give the overall seminar a focus, with each participant's work contributing to the overall focus.

As the teacher, constructively criticize presentations and raise questions that allow participants to see new dimensions and depth to what they are studying.

Use this approach when you need a reporting device for learners conducting original research.

Encourage seminar participants to raise questions and make comments following each formal presentation.

Avoid

Not allowing sufficient time for discussion and critique following formal presentations.

Allowing topics to range away from teacher's knowledge.

Not having a clear focus for the seminar.

Allowing one or two seminar members to take over the discussion.

SIMULATED TV SHOW

This teaching tool, which is an adaptation of role playing, can be used with good success. Participants like to do it, and I believe they gain much from it.

In small groups of three to five, I ask participants to plan a simulated television show of from five to seven minutes around an assigned topic. For example, if the class is studying major authors in a literature course, they might be asked to portray one of the authors. Each small group might portray the same author, or each small group could portray a different author.

The same approach could be used to illustrate a business management theory, a historical event, world trade issues, or a contemporary societal issue such as understanding the homeless.

Tips for Using

Provide background reading and other information sources to the class prior to the session where they will do the simulated TV show.

Divide the class into small groups of five to six. Counting off works well so that the small groups are formed by chance.

Suggest the following to each small group:

a. Discuss the information about the topic (person, historical event) and come to some common agreement (or identify areas of disagreement) about the available information.

b. Select a type of television show: game show, soap opera, news broadcast, documentary, situation comedy, detective show, or western that they wish to simulate.

Give each small group about one hour for the discussion and the development of the TV show.

After one hour, ask each group, in turn, to present its show in approximately five to seven minutes.

After each presentation, ask questions: What main points were you communicating? What difficulties did you have in deciding what ideas to communicate and how to communicate them?

Upon completion of all the presentations, discuss common themes presented by all the groups. Ask questions: Were you able to understand the person, event, or topic, at a level beyond reading or hearing about it? Assuming you were, what were some of the dimensions of this deeper level? What did you learn personally from this activity? Did you find this activity difficult? Were you uncomfortable with it? Why?

Avoid

Comparing the small groups with each other, implying some were of higher quality than others.

Rushing the process. Ample time must be provided for discussing the topic and developing the TV simulation.

Suggesting that everyone should be comfortable and excited about the process. Some participants will not be.

QUESTIONING

Being able to ask probing questions is one of the most powerful teaching tools. Asking questions can help participants dig more deeply into a topic or idea, explore various perspectives, and make thoughtful judgments about the accuracy and applications of information. Learners can examine in depth their own feelings and perspectives on a topic or issue.

Tips for Using

Use visuals such as chalkboard or newsprint to help record, organize, and synthesize answers.

Develop questions that can help people explore a topic more deeply, searching for accuracy and application:

- What is the source of this information?
- How do we know this source is accurate?
- How can we test the accuracy of this information?
- Do other sources differ with this source? In what way?
- Does this information square with your experience?
- Do we have all the information we need to develop a perspective on this topic? What appears to be missing?
- Do we have different interpretations of this information in this group? Explore people's interpretations.
- What applications do we see for this information?
- Where should this information not be applied?

Develop questions to assist people in exploring their own feelings and perspectives:

- How do you know this? Personal experience? Reading? Authority? Thought it through?
- Can you say more about this?
- Can you give me an example?

- How do you resolve your perspective with what X has said about this?

- How do you feel about this topic? Issue?

- If your position is this, can you describe the opposition to your position?

Avoid

Embarrassing people.

Arrogantly asking questions.

Pushing people too far. You can often tell by their body language when people are becoming extremely uncomfortable. Their eyes become glassy, and they rub their hands together and fold and unfold their fingers.

Moving people toward accepting your position on a question or issue. The purpose of questioning is to help people clarify *their* perspectives.

CONSCIOUSNESS RAISING

This tool can help participants examine something within their lives or in their communities that may not be immediately evident to them. The approach works best with a relatively small group of five to fifteen people. A larger group can be broken into smaller groups. For example, a group of parents could explore their children's elementary school's recreation program; a group of people in a community might examine the health resources available to them; or a group of citizens might look into problems with recycling solid wastes in their neighborhood.

For most groups, an action phase follows the initial meetings. That is, people try out what they are learning. Then the group comes back together again to discuss how well what they tried worked. They reexamine what they have discussed previously, reflect on the action steps they took, and then try again.

Tips for Using

Use a process such as the following. The example is for a group of professional people exploring their jobs.

1. Break the total group into smaller groups if the group is larger than fifteen people.

2. Ask participants each to write down what they do on a typical Wednesday (individual effort).

3. Ask participants to share what they have written. They make a list representing what each participant has said. The list is written on newsprint and taped to the wall for all to see.

4. When step 3 is completed, ask participants each to write down what they believe are the expectations of their jobs (individual effort).

5. Ask participants once again to share what they have written. They again make a list that represents what each participant has said. This list, too, is written on newsprint and taped to the wall alongside the previous list.

6. Discuss with the group the contradictions between the two lists.

7. Discuss the reasons (causes) for the contradictions. List them on newsprint and fasten the list alongside the other two lists.

8. Ask participants what actions they can take to correct the contradictions. Which of these actions can they take on Monday? Write these on newsprint and tape to the wall.

9. When the group meets at a later time, discuss the results of the efforts attempted and make decisions about further efforts.

Avoid

Putting your interpretation on what the contradictions are and what actions ought to be taken.

Making light of what people have written.

Allowing statements to be placed on newsprint that are not understood by each group member.

SEARCHING FOR ASSUMPTIONS

Teachers need ways of helping learners explore the foundations for their ideas and other people's ideas by identifying assumptions. I have used this tool in association with other teaching tools—for example, during a group discussion on a reading assignment or in a seminar.

Tips for Using

Take time to explain what an assumption is, and give examples of assumptions from written material so people are comfortable with the process.

When discussing written material, a film, or videotape, or a person's contributions in a group, ask, "What are the assumptions behind these statements, pictures, images?" Possible areas for exploration include: assumptions about people and their motivation, about government and its operations, about society and its purposes, about competition and cooperation, about progress equalling material possession, about who controls decision making in a society, and so on.

Avoid

Being impatient when people have difficulty ferreting out assumptions. The process does take some time, particularly when people have not done it before.

Presenting your own assumptions in such a way so you leave the impression that they are the right ones.

DEBATE

In those situation where I want to help participants clearly see two sides to an issue or question, I have often used a debate. I assign position A to a group of three to five persons within the larger group and assign position B to a group of similar size. Groups A and B are asked to make as strong a case as they can for their positions. Debate works best for groups of ten to thirty.

Tips for Using

Form groups by counting off or some other approach that mixes people.

Assign a position on a question or issue to each group. If you have four groups of five each, two groups will have the same position. For instance, if the discussion is about the issue of agricultural pesticides, two groups are assigned position A: "All agricultural pes-ticides should be banned," and two groups are assigned position B: "Agricultural pesticides are necessary for the future of world food production."

Give each group about fifteen minutes to develop its presentation.

Ask the first group (A) to present its position taking no longer than five minutes. Alert one of the opposing groups (B) to be prepared to rebut.

After Group A gives its presentation, the rebuttal group has three minutes to develop its rebuttal.

The rebuttal group presents its rebuttal for no more than two min-utes.

Repeat so that all groups have an opportunity to make both their primary presentations as well as rebuttals.

Discuss what was learned from the exercise when the presentations and rebuttals are completed.

Avoid

Allowing some groups to have more time than others in presentation or rebuttal.

TOOLS FOR OFFERING MULTIPLE PERSPECTIVES

PANEL

I've used this approach often at workshops and conferences where participants need to see several points of view on a topic. I ask three to five people of different perspectives and backgrounds to present their views on a question to a group. I usually serve as moderator of the panel, trying to make sure that none of the panelists dominates the discussion.

I follow the panel discussion with a variety of approaches, depend-ing on the amount of time, the kind of room, and the size of the audience. If there are movable chairs, I break the audience into smaller groups and follow a buzz group or group discussion approach. If time is short, and chairs are fixed, I may use the diad or triad approach in order to get reaction to the panel. These teaching tools are discussed earlier in this chapter.

If the audience is relatively small, say thirty people or less, asking the audience to raise questions directly with the panel can be effective.

Tips for Using

Select panelists who can easily and quickly make their points.

Give the panelists clear instructions with the expectation that they will be prepared.

Avoid

Allowing one panelist to dominate.

Allowing a few audience members to dominate.

Allowing the discussion to take place only among the panelists without any audience involvement.

GUEST SPEAKER

If you are teaching a class that meets several times, using a guest speaker is a good way of bringing another perspective to your group. Guest speakers can add an in-depth perspective to a topic, give another perspective on the topic, or describe a way of applying the subject matter.

A guest speaker may be followed with a forum, group discussion, or questions and answers.

Tips for Using

Ask the speaker for permission to audio or video record the presentation for persons who must miss the session or for use at other sessions.

If possible, check to see how well the potential guest speaker has been received by other groups.

In a letter to the guest speaker, outline specifically what you want covered, how much time you have available, and a description of the class's purpose and its members.

Be explicit about the details—date, time, place (with directions for finding the building, room).

Explain where the speaker should park.

Prior to the appearance, agree if a fee is involved.

Once the speaker has agreed to speak and you have sent the detailed information explained above, contact the speaker to see if there are any questions. You may want to meet with the speaker if the person is from the community.

Find out if the speaker needs audiovisual materials, flip chart, chalkboard, or other equipment.

If the speaker is bringing handouts, make certain there are enough copies for everyone.

Prepare your group for the speaker. Discuss why the speaker is coming, something about his or her background, and whether the participants should be prepared with questions.

Avoid

Using an excessive number of guest speakers, unless you are prepared to provide the continuity necessary for your participants.

Making a last minute selection of guest speakers that precludes carrying out the steps outlined above.

DRAWING

Learners are accustomed to expressing themselves with words, but sometimes, important ideas or feelings are best expressed in other ways. Drawing is one way to do that. Drawing also helps learners discover elements about themselves that they didn't know were there.

I've also found drawing a useful tool to help learners translate complex abstract ideas into a concrete presentation of what they understand. For example, I may ask participants in a study skills workshop to draw a picture of themselves as learners. Not only do learners wrestle with their own knowledge of themselves as learners, but they have an opportunity to see the wide variation in how others see themselves as learners.

Tips for Using

Give each participant a large sheet of paper—newsprint or flip chart paper works well—and marking pens or crayons.

Have masking tape available so the pictures may be displayed on the wall.

Give participant about fifteen to twenty minutes to complete their pictures. Suggest that participants who finish early might want to view pictures of other participants who have finished early.

Insist that participants use no words in their pictures.

When all of the pictures are on the wall, move as a group from picture to picture, asking the "artist" to say something about the picture—what it depicts and the difficulties in creating it.

Encourage group members to ask questions of each "artist."

When the exercise is complete, lead a discussion about the meaning of the exercise and what participants believe they learned.

Avoid

Making judgments about either the quality of the drawings or the ideas expressed.

Letting the group judge the drawings. Insist that they attempt to understand and appreciate what each "artist" has done.

3-D CREATION

Making three-dimensional creations is a powerful tool for uncovering knowledge participants may not know they have. As in drawing, this method allows learners to translate abstract ideas into concrete representations. This method also indirectly teaches cooperation and idea sharing.

For example, I ask learners in my classes to make 3-D creations of adult learning theories. You could use this approach for almost any abstract idea: labor-management relationships, theories of world trade, approaches to family relationships, and so on. Most participants (not all) have lots of fun doing this exercise.

I break my class or workshop group into smaller groups (three to five members) and ask them to create a 3-D representation of an abstract idea by using common office supplies such as tape, paper clips, paper, marking pens, envelopes, or easily available material such as paper cups and plates, fabric, and boxes.

Tips for Using

Give each small group an envelope with supplies that may be used for the creation. Give each group the same inventory of supplies.

Allow each group about an hour to discuss and construct a 3-D creation of the idea they have been assigned. Suggest they might want to spend about half of their time discussing, the other half constructing.

Encourage groups that finish early to view creations of other groups that finish early.

When all groups are finished, or time is called, move everyone from creation to creation while a representative of the group explains problems in building the creation, what ideas the creation represents, and the ideas the group discussed.

Lead a group discussion of problems people experienced with this method and what was learned from it.

Avoid

Making negative comments about the creations.

Allowing some groups to take an excessive amount of time to complete their creations while other group members are waiting.

CHAPTER 10

Teaching Tools for Creating a Good Learning Environment

The teaching tools in this chapter are designed for first and last sessions, developing a group agenda for your class, adding special interest, and helping individual learners with personal problems they may be facing.

Before looking at these tools, I want to say a word about the importance of humor in your teaching.

HUMOR

Unlike other teaching tools, humor doesn't stand alone but is always incorporated with other teaching tools.

Humor in the classroom can serve several functions. It can liberate creative capacity by offering novelty and helping learners break out of ruts. Humor can also help learners see that mistakes are a normal part of the learning process and are something at which all can laugh.

Likewise, you can become more human by laughing at those times when you commit an "oops." Humor can help you build relationships with learners, and relationships between and among learners result in a learning community. A humorous story or event that occurred in a class often provides a "hook" for remembering some important content. Humor can help to reduce tension in a classroom, especially when the subject matter is difficult or controversial and learners are feeling tense or overwrought. Humor helps calm emotions and relax learners so they can concentrate more fully. And lastly, humor often opens the lines to you and your learners by showing that you are human (Davies, 1989, p. 8).

I use humor all the time in my teaching. I wish I could tell you how to do it. I know what doesn't work. Don't bring in some story you read in a magazine or heard over the radio or, worse, picked up at a party the point of which has no relationship to your subject. It is absolutely taboo to attempt humor by poking fun at some ethnic, religious, or racial group. Humor is not humor when it demeans someone. It is not funny when you attempt humor at the expense of someone in your class or workshop, someone who is picking up an idea more slowly, or makes a mistake.

I use puns—participants sometimes groan, but they work. I often poke fun at myself, some mistake I've made, something from my experience that is relevant to the topic. Humor is an extremely personal thing. How you use it is very much a part of you. Experiment with it. If it doesn't work, it doesn't. Some people are probably not meant to be funny. But I think most of us have a humorous streak within us, and I believe most learners do too.

TOOLS FOR FIRST SESSIONS

ATMOSPHERE CREATORS

The atmosphere you create during the first hour of a class or workshop often determines the tone for the remainder of the class sessions or the workshop. The following tools are useful for establishing a positive atmosphere.

Tips for Using

Arrange the chairs in a circle so everyone can see everyone else, if the group has twenty-five or fewer members. If there are more than twenty-five participants, sitting around tables helps to reduce formality.

Greet participants at the door when they come to the first session. Introduce yourself. Give each participant a handout that briefly describes you, your background, and your experience with the content of the course or workshop.

Give participants, as they enter the room, a copy of the course or workshop syllabus or agenda. This should include objectives for the course or workshop, assignments and deadlines, grading procedures (if a credit course), suggested readings, suggested topics for each session, and where participants can buy required reading materials.

If appropriate, begin the session by going through the course agenda, elaborating on it and answering questions that participants may have about requirements, deadlines, and so on.

For many courses or workshops, allow participants to add topics they particularly want to have covered. This can be done following a discussion of the agenda or during the time that participants introduce themselves. Write the additional topics on the chalkboard. Indicate whether you will or will not be able to cover the additional topic requests—so participants know what is in store for them (see Chapter 13). For some workshops you may want to concentrate entirely on what the participants want to do within a broad topic area. See "Tools For Developing a Group Agenda" below.

Indicate when the participants can anticipate breaks. No session should go longer than forty-five or fifty minutes without a ten-minute break. Provide directions to restrooms and vending machines.

Provide something eminently practical during the first time the course or workshop meets. This can be a new skill or a new piece of usable information. A handout may be distributed that includes a description of this new skill or new information. An example in a beginning computer course would be how to turn on the computer and bring the software on line. Whatever it is, make sure the participants have the experience of actually learning something.

INTRODUCTIONS

Take time during the first session for participants to get to know each other. Here are several approaches.

Tips for Using

Ask participants to interview the person next to them for five minutes. Then switch and the second person interviews the first. Ask the people in each pair to introduce each other to the group giving names, hometowns, avocational interests, and workplaces. To add interest, ask people to find out from their partners something they did within the past six months that was particularly exciting for them, and share this with the class.

Go through the months asking persons with birthdays during the month mentioned to give their names, and so on. Ask for the same information as above.

If the group is seated at tables, provide stand-up name tags. Participants can make these from five-by-seven cards that are folded the long way.

Provide name tags for participants to wear, particularly during the first session. Make sure the writing on tags is large enough to be seen. For sessions when you do not know the names ahead of time, have participants make their own name tags when they arrive.

When using small group discussion, ask that participants reintroduce themselves to their small group before beginning the discussion.

TOOLS FOR DEVELOPING A GROUP AGENDA

GROUP WORKSHOP PLANNING PROCESS

Here is a group process for identifying learner needs and interests, but with an emphasis on individually developed statements. The process is designed for learning sessions where the major attention of the session is on the topics (needs and interests) expressed by the group participants (Adapted from Delbecq, Van de Ven & Gustafson, 1975).

Tips for Using

Divide the total group into smaller groups of five to seven. Each group should have paper and pencil for each member, a flip chart, a felt pen, and masking tape.

1. Instruct each person to take a few moments to think about questions or topics that should be covered in the workshop.

2. Ask participants to independently list their questions or topics for the workshop. Ask them not to talk with other participants during the thinking and writing process.

3. When steps 1 and 2 are completed, instruct each small group to select one person as recorder.

4. Go around the table and have each person read one of the questions or topics. The recorder writes this question or topic on the flip

chart in brief words or phrases. The recorder takes a turn with the rest of the participants. Continue around the group, each member in turn, until all the topics and questions are listed. People without further questions or topics are passed over. When a sheet is filled, tape it to the wall for the small group's reference.

5. Discuss each question or topic in turn so everyone can understand what has been written.

6. Ask each small group member to write on a separate sheet of paper the five items from those posted on the wall he or she considers most important. Once each person has completed this task, ask each member to assign a value of "5" to the most important item, a "4" to the next important on to a "1" as least important. The recorder should then write these votes on the flip chart.

For example, if the group selects six items from its list, the voting might appear as follows:

Item	Votes	Total	Rank
3	1-3-1-2-3	10	4
5	1-3-2-2	8	5
6	2-3-1-2-3	11	3
7	5-5-5-4-4	23	1
10	5-4-4-5-4	22	2
12	1-2	3	6

7. Collect the flip charts from each group showing the results of its deliberations and voting for the total group to see. Indicate that unless there is substantial disagreement, the highest ranked questions will receive the most attention in the workshop.

Be aware of two cautions I have discovered. First, participants, once they begin studying, discussing, and becoming more aware of a topic, may change their minds about what is most important for them. Even though they may have told you, through this process, what they wanted included in the workshop, they will likely adjust their thinking as the workshop progresses. Second, if the topic of the workshop is not familiar to the participants, they may not know what questions to ask or what the possible topics are. Thus, you as teacher must take the leadership for introducing new topics and questions that take learners beyond their present questions and topics of interest.

BRAINSTORMING

Brainstorming is a good approach for identifying many ideas in a short time. I've used it to list quickly the questions and topics that participants want to study. After the initial list is completed, the items can be discussed and given a priority following a voting procedure as described in the Group Workshop Planning Process above. The group can also use a freewheeling approach where someone tosses out an idea, the teacher draws a circle around it, and people offer related ideas in a webbing fashion (see Chapter 13).

Tips for Using and What To Avoid

Explain the process. Within a group of ten to fifteen members each person blurts out questions or topics while the recorder writes on a flip chart or chalkboard as quickly as possible the essence of each comment.

Set a definite time for idea creation. Three to five minutes works well.

Ask for clarification and understanding of each topic or question, but avoid judging merits of any item during the idea creation phase.

Ask each person to rank five items and accord point values (5 for first, 4 for second, 3 for third, 2 for fourth, 1 for fifth—same as for the Group Workshop Planning Process as explained above). You now have an initial list of what the participants consider to be the main topics and questions they wish to have covered in the course. The same cautions as for the Group Workshop Planning Process apply.

TOOLS TO ADD INTEREST

POTLUCK MEAL/SNACKS

For those classes that meet several times over a month or more, a potluck meal can add an interesting social dimension to the group. I suggest learners invite their spouses or friends. The meal can be held immediately after one of the class sessions or during the dinner break for those classes that normally meet in the late afternoon and evening. A committee from the class can take charge of the planning and arrangements.

For classes that meet over the lunch hour or over dinner, participants may take turns bringing snacks to each class.

ALTERNATIVE CLASSROOM

If a class meets in the same room for six or more times, a interesting break is to move the class to another room for at least one time. For example, if the class has been meeting in a library conference room, moving the class to someone's home for one meeting offers a break in the routine and can help renew interest. Make certain that all members know where the alternative room is and that learners who miss the preceding session are informed of the changed meeting place.

TOOLS FOR LAST SESSIONS

LEARNING CELEBRATION

The last session can be as important as the first session for many courses and workshops, particularly those that meet several times. Traditionally, the last session for many courses (particularly credit courses) has been devoted to a final examination, an end-of-session form, and a rush to include information that you had intended to cover earlier.

Examinations and end-of-meeting forms are often necessary components of final sessions. But dumping previously not included information is seldom a good idea. Consider what else might be accomplished. Participants who have struggled with the material, shared in discussions, questioned each other, and in most instances, come to enjoy each other often feel let down when the class or workshop simply stops. So, the final session can be a "learning celebration."

Ways to celebrate can also include:

- A general discussion of the course upon completion of the end-of-meeting form—what went well, what should be changed. Have coffee and cookies or other refreshments for this session.

- A dinner at a nearby restaurant following the end-of-session forms and other necessary chores.

- A potluck dinner or a party/open house at someone's home. Some instructors enjoy hosting such events.

TOOLS FOR INDIVIDUAL PROBLEM SOLVING

STUDY GROUP

I have encouraged learners to form study groups for those classes that continue over several weeks and deal with topics that are quite new or difficult for learners. A study group consists of from three to five learners who meet regularly outside of class to discuss class content, share individual problems, prepare for examinations (when they are part of the class), and assist each other to learn.

Tips for Using and What To Avoid

Wait to form study groups until the class has met two or three times and the participants have become acquainted.

Allow learners to form their own study groups, but encourage them to include people in their groups who may think differently than they do. Such diversity can help learning.

Be alert to help those who have difficulty finding a group.

Encourage everyone to be part of a study group, if you are using this method. Those not a part of a study group will increasingly feel left out as the course proceeds.

Be available to meet with study groups, if they request your assistance, but do not meet regularly with them—you may be the problem they want to discuss.

INDIVIDUAL CONFERENCE

Make yourself available for meetings with participants before class, after class, over coffee, in your office—wherever convenient for you and the learner. The individual conference allows learners to ask you questions they may have been uncomfortable raising in front of the entire class.

Tips for Doing and What To Avoid

Be available for learners who want to talk with you away from the meeting room.

If the conference is based on an appointment, make every effort to keep the appointment or notify the learner if the conference time must be changed.

Be alert to personal problems that are clearly beyond your competency for handling. Have available names of people to whom the learner can be referred.

Be a good listener. Avoid making judgments about the learner's responses or questions.

Try to help the learner work out problems by raising questions and offering alternative solutions.

Be honest but also careful about responding to questions about "How am I doing?" Too critical a response given in a perceived noncaring way may drive the participant away from your class.

SELF-CONFIDENCE BUILDING

Adults often come to a workshop or course with low confidence in themselves and their ability to succeed. This is particularly so in those workshops and classes that deal with such topics as improving study skills, improving writing, and sharpening public speaking abilities. Here is a tool to help build self-confidence (Adapted from Apps, 1990).

Tips for Using and What To Avoid

Divide the class into small groups of three or four participants each.

Ask participants to share with others in their group a success, accomplishment, or achievement they experienced before they were twelve years old, between the ages of twelve and twenty, and between twenty and the present time. This need not be a grand and publicly recognized achievement, but something that was important to the participant.

Repeat the process but this time ask the participants to share their greatest successes during the past month and the past week.

With the whole group, discuss any difficulties that participants may have had in carrying out the assignment. Were there surprises concerning how many successes people were able to recall?

Discuss intentions for feeling successful in the course in which participants are enrolled. Include ways to set goals and make plans for reaching them.

CHAPTER 11

Selecting the Right Tool

You have the choice of many teaching tools, ranging from lecturing to debate, interactive computer to buzz groups, case study to simulation games, and much more. The following considerations will help you decide which tool to use.

1. The objectives for the class or workshop

2. The characteristics of the participants

3. The subject matter

4. The characteristics of the teaching tools: what a particular tool will do and what it will not do

5. The learning situation: the type of meeting room and any potential distractions

6. The teaching tools you prefer

Let's look at each of these areas in more detail.

THE OBJECTIVES

What is the purpose of your class or workshop? What are the participants supposed to gain from it? The teaching tools in the previous three chapters are organized according to anticipated purposes. For instance, to emphasize an in-depth understanding of a content area, for example the politics of the Middle East, tools for in-depth understanding, multiple perspectives, and perhaps tools for providing information could be applied.

Some tools to foster in-depth understanding include the following:
Buzz Group
Diad and Triad
Forum
Group Discussion
Group Project
Quiet Meeting
Role Playing
Seminar
Simulation Game
Some tools for developing multiple perspectives include the following:
Drawing
Guest Speaker
Panel
Simulated TV Show
3-D Creation
Useful tools for providing information include:
Field Trip
Interview
Lecture
Print Materials
Result Demonstration
If you plan to focus attention on developing critical thinking skills, see Chapter 12 for an in-depth discussion.

THE CHARACTERISTICS OF LEARNERS

Groups of adults generally differ in age, educational level, experience, learning style preference, and personal history. You obviously can't select teaching tools that fit the unique needs and interests of each person, but knowing about the people in your group, in several dimensions, can help you select appropriate teaching tools.

Knowing the amount of experience or information group members have about the subject when they begin can help you select appropriate tools. If the group has limited knowledge and experience about the topic, don't immediately begin a group discussion. Use tools for providing information as a beginning place. Later you can use tools that develop in-depth understanding, offer multiple perspectives, and present opportunity for critical thinking.

Are there persons with hearing or vision problems? Be particularly mindful of this in your use of audiovisual aids.

Are people attending the workshop or course by choice, or must they attend, for example, to maintain certification or to earn credits for salary increases? Some compulsory attenders will participate readily to make sure they receive proper credit for their attendance; others will participate reluctantly, if at all.

Is there generally high personal motivation—a writing course where everyone wants to publish, for example? Highly motivated learners will participate in a range of activities with little hesitancy.

What is the range of basic skills in writing, reading, speaking, and listening? If several participants lack basic communication skills, you may be limited in your choices of some tools or it will take longer to accomplish certain tasks.

Which learning styles do the participants prefer? You will likely have considerable diversity. Even though adults tend to prefer one learning style over another, particular circumstances (content studied, what the participant already knows in a subject area, and so on) will influence which learning style the participant will prefer at any one time. Many adults, when exposed to teaching approaches new to them, become quite comfortable and often say they are learning more than they do from approaches that seem more allied with their preferred learning styles. Refer to the References section for books describing learning style inventories and their use.

From my experience, I believe most adult learners fall into one of three learning style categories. Below are descriptions of each category with some suggestions for appropriate teaching tools.

Intuitive Learners

Intuitive learners:

Prefer learning when both feeling and thinking are combined.

Want to find meaning for themselves in what is presented.

Resent having a teacher tell them what they should learn and how they should learn it.

Like to make their own judgments about how they can apply what they are learning.

Appreciate getting to know other learners as people and for the knowledge fellow learners have to share.

Some appropriate tools for intuitive learners include:

Buzz Group

Drawing

Group Discussion
Guest Speaker
Lecture
Print Materials
Quiet Meeting
Role Playing
Simulated TV Show
Study Group
3-D Creation

Sequential Learners

Sequential learners:
Appreciate carefully planned learning experiences where they know exactly what is to be learned and how they should learn it.
Prefer to learn things in order, first this, then this. Each thing learned builds on the previous information.
Are more concerned with facts than with feelings.
Tools for teaching sequential learners include:
Interactive Computer
Lecture
Print Materials

Practical Learners

Practical learners:
Want fast-paced teaching that has immediate application.
Have little patience for "Getting Acquainted" teaching tools and other activities which foster a sense of community.
Prefer teaching approaches that use examples directly applicable to their situation.
Have little time for what they perceive as theoretical material unless they can see immediate application to practice.
Some tools that practical learners find useful include:
Case Study
Group Project
Internship
Result Demonstration
Skill Demonstration
Simulation Game

THE SUBJECT MATTER

If you are teaching woodworking skills, you wouldn't spend an entire workshop lecturing. Hands-on experience is required. Likewise, you wouldn't ask a swimming class to spend its time watching video tapes of outstanding swimmers (although this might be a part of the course); you would move them into the pool.

For other subject matter, the teaching tools to use are less obvious. A workshop dealing with environmental issues might require some combination of tools to teach multiple perspectives, indepth understanding, and critical thinking.

THE CHARACTERISTICS OF THE TEACHING TOOLS

If you have sessions that are only an hour, you obviously can't use some of the tools that take longer, such as 3-D Creation, or Simulation Game. Not only must you consider the time it takes to use a particular tool in a class or workshop, you must also factor in the amount of preparation time. For instance, if you plan to write your own case study or simulation, then you must obviously plan considerable preparation time.

How difficult is the tool to use? Will it take considerable time to explain? A debate can be complicated to explain and administer the first time it is used. Using certain computer simulations can be difficult, particularly if learners have had little experience with computers.

THE LEARNING SITUATION

Location has a great influence on what tools you can and cannot use. If your meeting room has fixed chairs, you will have obvious problems using small group discussion (with the exception of diads and triads). If the room has an unusual shape, you may also be limited. I recall teaching a workshop several years ago where the meeting room was a library. The room was divided in half, in the shape of a V. My position was at the bottom of the V where I could see people in each leg of the V, but they couldn't see each other. It was like working with two different groups at the same time—even though I was trying to do the same thing with each. In many ways it was an impossible situation, except for straight lecturing, which is what those who brought me in expected me to do.

Group size affects choice of teaching tools usually only when the group is larger than twenty-five to forty. For instance, if your group is larger than twenty-five do not expect to do much whole group discussion. But with movable chairs, considerable small group discussion is possible. I have seen effective small group discussion, around tables, with groups as large as two hundred. I also once observed a presenter attempting to use small group discussion with a group of twelve hundred people in a huge banquet hall and it was a disaster.

Groups larger than twenty-five to forty also prevent the use of most experiential approaches such as 3-D Creation, Drawing, Consciousness Raising, and Searching for Assumptions, unless you have help. Even with assistants, the management of experiential learning projects with large groups can quickly become overpowering.

Time of day influences the choice of tools. Work-weary participants coming to your class at day's end often require teaching tools that excite and involve. A long boring lecture will promptly lull them to sleep, unless the topic is riveting. Consider using a variety of tools and changing the pace fairly often.

The *length of the sessions* influences which tools you choose. An all day workshop provides a great opportunity for trying a variety of teaching tools, while an hour-long session is considerably more confining. Even with the latter, however, you can use far more variety than you might imagine. You may comfortably use Diad and Triad, Buzz Group, Group Discussion, Role Playing, Debate, or Demonstration, for example.

THE TEACHER'S PREFERENCE

Teachers often prefer the tools they use well. Good speakers like to lecture. Some enjoy using audiovisual equipment. Teachers who like working out elaborate management schemes will probably choose complicated learner involvement tools.

But what if the tools you are most comfortable with are not the ones that best fit the criteria listed above? Do you blindly go on, or do you cultivate the use of new tools? A leather carver who needs to learn how to use a new tool in order to carve letters either decides to not carve letters or learns how to use the new tool. In many situations you may not have a choice. If you avoid learning how to use new tools, participants won't return to your classes or workshops.

One approach is to consciously decide that you are going to learn how to use some new tools during the coming year. Select those tools that best fit the factors listed above and are interesting to you. Think how the tool might be used at a particular time in your class or workshop.

Then try it with your class. If you are a little nervous about the tool and your performance with it, announce to the group that you haven't done this before. Most groups will rally around you and enjoy the new approach to learning, and they will give you constructive feedback about how to improve your use of the tool.

Master teachers constantly push beyond their present limits of performance. This means taking risks, trying new ideas, examining what worked right and what didn't, and then trying it again. In this way, your bag of teaching tools will ever increase. You will feel that you are constantly growing as a teacher, not having to rely forever on old teaching tools that can become a little stale in the doing.

A risk for trying new things is failure. To move on from where you are now, you need to accept failure, learn from it, and go forward. The joy in trying new approaches is in the satisfaction that you are learning and growing as you teach.

THE ART OF SELECTING AND USING TOOLS

It makes sense to consider the above factors when selecting tools for different teaching situations. It also makes sense to plan what teaching tools you will use during a given teaching session. But in addition to being rational and systematic, there is also an artful dimension to tool selection. Master teachers have a "feeling" about a group, the subject matter, and the circumstances that surround it. Master teachers, often without being able to explain why, select a particular teaching tool because they believe it will be the best one to accomplish a given purpose. And they are often right.

In addition master teachers blend teaching tools during the course of a teaching session. Some blending can obviously be preplanned, but not all. A master teacher knows when to move from one teaching tool to another, from lecturing to group discussion, from a simulation game to questioning for critical thinking. You will learn when to abandon a tool that is not working with a particular group and move to another. You will also learn to "read" a group, as it progresses through various learning exercises and know when to stop, when to continue, when to suggest a break, and when to use a different tool. Some clues to watch for include body language (shuffling around in seats, paging through notes) and looks of confusion or boredom.

Art influences in a large way how well a particular tool is used. The same tool, used by two different teachers with the same group, same subject matter, same room, can be an unqualified disaster for one teacher and a huge success for another. The difference between how the two teachers used the tool is often not easy to identify. A certain subtleness and elegance can make the difference. The master teacher has that something extra, the edge that defines the difference between acceptability and greatness. It involves proper selection of tools, but is much deeper and more profound. Master teachers are constantly searching for the edge that defines greatness. They know it when they have it, and their participants know it as well. One way to develop it is to watch master teachers in action. Another approach is to videotape your own teaching, and then watch your performance with a master teacher offering a critique. This edge that makes the difference between average teaching and greatness can be learned, but I can't tell you exactly how to do it. In a sense, each master teacher is challenged to develop this something extra that makes each teacher unique and special.

CHAPTER 12

Teaching Critical Thinking

The day is past when we can say we have taught when we have given people information or have shown them how to do something. Learners are demanding more. They want to understand information; they want to see how it relates to what they already know and are able to do. They often want assistance in sorting out the huge chunks of information they have access to, to see what fits their situation. Many want to look beneath what they are learning, to understand what the ideas really mean and the context from which these ideas come.

In our complex world, people want to regain control of their lives, their jobs, their communities, and their government. Critical thinking skills can help them to do this.

As a teacher, you have an obligation to help people develop skills for critical thinking. For some people, this may be an unpleasant experience. Some learners will resent your initial attempts to encourage questioning and new ways of looking at things. They may be comfortable depending on someone else to tell them what to do and how to do it. You have an obligation to help those who are comfortable become uncomfortable. Likewise, through critical thinking skills, you can help those who are uncomfortable about their lives, their work, and their world become more comfortable. My particular approach to the process of critical thinking is closely related to learning for transformation, or transformative education.

I learned how to teach critical thinking over many years of practice. Early in my career as a teacher of adults I began offering workshops and short courses. Participants seemed to enjoy and gain from what I was doing, but I had a nagging feeling that something was missing, that participants wanted and deserved more.

Then, one weekend, I was teaching a workshop for rural mental health workers who worked with large numbers of rural poor. The work-

95

shop focused on how to identify goals, set priorities, and develop practical strategies for working with rural poor.

I had many ideas about these topics because I had recently completed a graduate program. On the other hand, these mental health workers had heard about all the facts and theories concerning goals, priorities, and strategies they could stomach. After an hour or so, they politely told me they wanted something different. We then moved from my lecture setting with appropriate overhead visuals to a workshop setting where they and I became totally immersed. Together, we examined their work setting, and they helped me understand what they did and how they did it. They told me about their dreams, and we wrote them on newsprint and taped them to the walls. They reported on what blocked their dreams, and we taped this information on the walls.

Then we began discussing how to overcome the blocks—the specific strategies to use. I dug deep into the recesses of my experience and training to share what I knew, and they shared with each other and with me what they knew. At the end of the second day we were all exhausted, but elated. I had experienced a new way of teaching, and of learning.

Over the years, I have polished this approach to teaching, applying it with many groups in many settings, and with a variety of topics.

TEACHING FOR CRITICAL THINKING

I've discovered that teaching critical thinking is an attitude the teacher has. It becomes a part of you in almost everything you do. Thus you can apply elements of critical thinking in a variety of situations.

For example, I remember a participant in my writing class at the Rhinelander School of Arts, in Rhinelander, Wisconsin. On the first day of the week-long workshop, she cornered me and said, "I have but one reason for being in your class. I want you to show me how to sell what I have written. Don't bore me with material on how to write, I want to learn how to sell."

That's not a particularly unreasonable request. Many writers seek publication of their work with appropriate compensation. I asked if she had any material that she had been trying to sell. She handed me a folder containing several short pieces of her writing.

That evening I read over her material and quickly learned why editors had filled her mail box with rejection slips. The material was simply not ready for publication. My challenge was to help her see her work in a new light, to see that focusing on improving writing ought to come before attending to problems of marketing. But what teaching strategy could I use to help her see this? I considered the alternatives. I could simply tell her flat out that her work wasn't ready for publication. For some people that might work, but for her I'd probably hear, "You don't understand the power of my work; you're just like the editors I've contacted so far."

One of the pieces was supposedly humorous. I decided that during the next session of the workshop I'd ask her to read the piece to the entire group. I usually asked three or four participants to share their work every day, so I wasn't singling her out. After the reading, I broke the total group into work groups of four or five people to critique what they had heard and offer suggestions for improvement.

She read the humorous piece to the group. Dead silence. Not a chuckle, not a giggle, not even a smile. I watched the color leave her face, but said nothing. After the small groups had discussed her article for a few minutes, each group offered a list of ideas for improving the article. She took notes, but said nothing, and we went on to the next person.

After the session, she stormed by me without saying a word, and I was afraid she might drop the workshop. But she didn't. She was back the next day, looking like she hadn't slept the previous night.

After that day's session she said to me, "Would you look at a revision of my work?"

"Sure," I replied.

It was considerably improved, but still needed more work, and she eagerly accepted my suggestions when we talked after class.

What had happened? She had learned how to look critically at her own work, but not until after she had become aware that her focus was in the wrong direction. She needed to improve her writing skills before she worried about marketing.

In the process of teaching critical thinking skills, I have often reflected on what teaching tools seemed to work better than others. Here is some of what I learned.

A PROCESS FOR CRITICAL THINKING

My approach to critical thinking includes these phases:

• Helping learners become aware

• Helping learners explore alternatives

• Helping learners work through a transition

- Helping learners achieve integration

- Helping learners take action (when appropriate)

Helping Learners Become Aware

Becoming aware is a process where you help learners to look at their needs and wants in often new and deeper ways. Becoming aware is also a process where you help learners to see needs, problems, and circumstances in their lives, their work, and their communities they have not been aware of before.

Some learners enroll in classes or workshops because of a crisis in their lives. They have lost their jobs, they are recently divorced or recently married, a spouse or close friend has died, they have been promoted and feel insecure, or the boss has rolled in a new machine and said "Everyone must know how to operate this before the end of the month." Awareness is not a problem for these people—they are keenly aware and want to quickly move into succeeding phases of learning.

Far more people in adult education are not so aware. I believe I have an obligation to help people see things in a deeper, more critical way. Generally, what I try to do when I help learners become aware is to help them examine the problems or questions they have about their work, their communities, or their lives. I help them make the usual, unusual; the ordinary, extraordinary; the common, uncommon.

I have found certain tools to be effective. Specific information about them can be found in Chapters 8, 9, and 10. Some appropriate tools for developing awareness are:

Case Study
Consciousness Raising
Debate
Drawing
Field Trip
Group Discussion
Internship
Questioning
Quiet Meeting
Role Playing
Searching for Assumptions
Simulated TV Show
3-D Creation

I have used all of these tools at one time or another with a large variety of groups. Some of the tools are serious and intense such as Searching for Assumptions and Consciousness Raising. Others, such as Drawing, 3-D Creation, Simulated TV Show, and Role Playing, can be fun and at the same time serve as powerful teaching tools for developing awareness.

Helping Learners Explore Alternatives

Once learners have developed a deeper awareness of their problem, question, or situation, they are ready to explore alternatives. These may be alternative answers to questions, alternative solutions to a problem, or alternative viewpoints on a controversial question.

A key principle for this phase of the critical thinking process is the ability to remain open to a wide range of perspectives before settling in on one solution, answer, or viewpoint. I often must keep encouraging people to look beyond the ideas they first uncover. When they think they have explored as far as they can go, then I push them to think beyond that.

Many of us tend to latch onto the first plausible idea we encounter. Critical thinking means being critical of all ideas that we encounter, inspecting them, looking at them from various perspectives, and above all, looking widely for them.

Encourage people to examine many sources of ideas, starting with what they already know but may not be aware that they know. Some of the awareness tools discussed above often not only help people become more aware, but also help them become more conscious of what they already know. Fellow learners are also an excellent source of ideas. You, the teacher, are of course an idea source as are reading materials and the host of other places where information is stored such as audio and video tapes and computer databases.

Often, during the process of exploring alternatives, learners run onto viewpoints, ways of doing things, or ideas that run counter to what they have long believed. This can become very uncomfortable for the learner, and leads us to the next phase of critical thinking—transition.

Helping Learners Work Through a Transition

Often, learners must work through which alternative solution, problem, answer, idea, or perspective they want to become their own. For most adults, this means leaving behind some long held idea or position, way of doing something, or even attitude toward something. Sometimes, for certain kinds of learning, the learner's basic assumptions and values are brought into question and the transition process becomes even more difficult.

Recently, a woman from nutrition science enrolled in my class on preparing teachers of adults. I noticed about a third of the way through the course that she was becoming extremely frustrated. I could tell by her comments and questions in class, and I could see frustration in her face. Finally, one day, she blurted out that almost everything I was covering in class and modeling in my teaching ran counter to what she believed and found important about teaching.

I asked her to explain. She said that for her a teacher was an expert on a given topic, and teaching meant sharing that expertise with the class. The only time learners asked questions was at the end of lectures and then only to clarify some point the teacher may have made. What right, she asked, do participants have to question teachers as participants in my class were doing? And why should participants be encouraged to share their own experiences and knowledge? Wasn't that merely a waste of time and a distraction?

As a class, we talked about this learner's concerns. I had heard them from many others over the years.

This learner was clearly experiencing the transition phase of critical thinking. She was wrestling with her own long standing beliefs and values about teaching and with the ideas and approaches being presented and encouraged in the class.

She was uncomfortable, not knowing which way to turn. Part of her was saying she liked what she was reading about, hearing, and experiencing in the class, but another part of her, a deeper longer standing part, was fighting with these new ideas. She was extremely uneasy about calling into question what she had long believed, and she didn't know what new guide she should acquire. She was considering leaving some old ways of thinking behind and was struggling with the pain of doing so.

W. Bridges (1980), the author of *Transitions*, wrote, "the reality that is left behind . . . is not just a picture on the wall. It is a sense of which way is up and which way is down; it is a sense of which way is forward and which is backward. It is, in short, a way of orienting oneself and of moving forward into the future. . . . The old sense of life as 'going somewhere' breaks down, and we feel like shipwrecked sailors on some existential atoll" (p. 102).

Once she decided on a new foundation for her thinking about teachers of adults, this woman then faced grieving the loss of her old set of beliefs. P. Marris (1974), author of *Loss and Change*, said "The more radical the changes which evolve [in the process of learning], the more important [it is to] recognize the element of bereavement . . . in the process of major reconstruction" (p. 151).

In my experience, grieving the loss of old ideas, of old perspectives and ways of thinking, of former beliefs and values, is a process not dissimilar from losing a loved one. The learner must have time to work through it.

In many of my classes I encourage learners to keep journals, just as I am encouraging journal writing for teachers. I encourage learners to write, in detail, what they are experiencing and what their feelings are about what they are experiencing. For many learners, putting in writing what is going on during this transition phase is a major step toward resolving the trauma transition can present. An important point to underline is that *transition takes time.*

I've also found several teaching tools which help learners work through the transition process, including grieving the loss of old ideas:

Consciousness Raising
Group Discussion
Group Project
Individual Conference
Quiet Meeting
Seminar
Study Group

Helping Learners Achieve Integration

Following the often tumultuous transition phase, the learner, in the integration phase, begins putting things back together again. Now the learner builds something new—a new idea about something, a different way of carrying out some skill, or a new view of information previously held. Sometimes, when basic values and beliefs are involved, the integration phase includes developing a position on new values and beliefs. Often, remnants from past thinking and positions are carried into the new formulation of ideas. The teaching tools suggested below can help learners see the social acceptability or even the plausibility of their new combinations of ideas and approaches.

The integration phase includes becoming comfortable with the new ideas, new assumptions, and new ways of thinking that emerged from the transition phase. This phase may occur over a long period of time, six months or more if basic assumptions and values are involved. In some instances, integration can occur very quickly. Learners know when integration has occurred because they feel better about their work and about themselves. A new sense of importance and meaning enters their lives, and they feel released from old pressures. These feelings are particularly evident in those cases when learners are dealing with more fundamental shifts in their thinking and believing.

For the integration phase to occur, many learners need time alone, to think and reflect about these new ideas and understandings they are putting together. Journal writing can be a powerful tool here, as it is during other phases of critical thinking. Other teaching tools that may help the integration phase include:

Consciousness Raising
Drawing
Group Discussion
Individual Conference
Quiet Meeting
Searching for Assumptions
Seminar
Study Group
3-D Creation

Some of the same tools used for the awareness phase such as Consciousness Raising, Searching for Assumptions, Drawing, and 3-D Creation can help learners begin to understand their new approaches to integrating ideas, beliefs, and values.

Helping Learners Take Action

Taking action means doing something with the new ideas. For example, the woman from my writing class that I mentioned at the beginning of this chapter begin working on improving her writing. It wasn't until she began acting on her changed perspective that the results of her critical thinking really made sense to her.

Sometimes the action phase doesn't immediately follow integration. For example, participants in a class on Native American Treaty Rights may not have an opportunity to act on their understanding until some time in the future when their state legislature debates the nature of these rights.

The action phase of critical thinking is a reality check on what was learned. Often, as a result of acting, a learner develops a new awareness, and the process may start over again.

CRITICAL THINKING NOT LINEAR

I must also point out, from my experience with several hundred learners who have worked through this process in my classes and workshops, that I have seen few work through the process in a step-by-step fashion.

For instance, some learners will work at the awareness phase, move to alternatives, and then develop a new awareness, before once more moving to alternatives. Some learners, in the transition phase, will develop a profoundly important awareness of something that had not occurred to them when they were in the awareness phase the first time, and they go back to the beginning of the process.

Even during integration, I have seen some learners develop new awareness and circle back to the starting phase. The point is, with any group of learners, it is possible to have people at all points in the process at any one time. This is both the excitement and the challenge of teaching critical thinking.

TIPS FOR TEACHING CRITICAL THINKING

Here are some practical ideas I have learned from teaching critical thinking.

General Suggestions

Seldom do I teach critical thinking as a separate topic. It is incorporated into all the classes and workshops I teach such as those on writing, on preparing teachers of adults, and on examining new directions for continuing education agencies and institutions. The only time I conduct workshops that directly focus on critical thinking is when I teach the process to other teachers. For instance, when I teach a workshop on life story writing, I am, in effect, teaching at two levels. I am teaching the skills for life story writing, and I am teaching critical thinking. My hope is that the skills for critical thinking will be those learners can use in many other situations in their lives, well beyond the immediate application— life story writing.

For learners to really learn critical thinking, they must experience it. I can tell you about the joys and the agony of the transition phase, and you may nod your head that you understand, but until you have gone through the transition phase you can't really know what it means.

For longer workshops (several days) or longer classes (four or more sessions) I usually explain something about the critical thinking process either during the last session or at both the first and last session. In those workshops and classes where I am clearly using the process as a way of analyzing a situation (such as a workshop on examining alternative pol-

icies for continuing education) I explain the process during the first session and refer to it often as the sessions progress. In my writing classes,
I will likely make mention of the process only during the final session,
as a way of illustrating what people have experienced so they might try
it in other situations.

For shorter workshops, (an hour or two) I may not even mention
the critical thinking process, and indeed, I may not expect learners to
move very far into the process. But I will help people examine the topic
I am dealing with in a critical way, even if there isn't time to work through
a critical thinking process.

As you might guess from earlier comments, the critical thinking process works best when there is time between sessions. I've seen it work well
in a three day workshop, and of course I've seen it work exceedingly well
with classes that meet once a week for five or six weeks.

Critical thinking requires that learners interact with you, the teacher,
and with each other. When I am giving a speech, I may provide some
information, and I may suggest ways people can look at ideas in different
ways. Even so, participants have a chance to question and challenge me
and have a chance to examine their own perspectives in relation to what
I've said, little critical thinking takes place.

Teaching designed with narrowly defined behavioral objectives or
tightly specified performance outcomes for learners seldom provides
much opportunity for critical thinking. Likewise, when teaching is defined as presenting information to learners, and teaching success is measured by how well learners do on objective tests, little critical thinking
takes place.

In my experience, participants in a class or workshop will not work
through the critical thinking process lock step. Some will remain at the
awareness phase while others will be thinking about action steps, and
there will be participants at every phase in between.

Also, because the process is not a linear one, participants will move
back and forth among the phases. I must confess that I sometimes don't
know where a person is in the process. I have seen many participants
wrestle with the transition phase and move back to awareness or back to
looking for more alternatives. Some participants will not move through
the entire process by the end of your course or workshop. All of this will
be a bit disconcerting for you, but such behavior goes with teaching critical
thinking.

I have also found it useful to do some critical thinking of my own
after each teaching session, reflecting on what worked and what didn't,
on which participants seemed to be having problems, and what I could
do to help, and what I would do differently during the following session.

Working Through the Process

Here are some reactions I have received from people while they work through the various phases of the critical thinking process.

Awareness. Some participants resist my attempts to help them see more broadly and examine their situations in greater depth. They tell me they came to solve a particular problem or meet some need they have, and they don't have time to "fool around with this other stuff." You'll have to decide how you want to work with people with these feelings. Once when I worked for University Extension, a farmer came to my office with the question, "How much silage does my silo hold?" He didn't want to know about new approaches to feeding, or the values of silage over other feeds, or whether he purchased the right kind of silo. He just wanted to know how much silage a silo 50 feet tall by 12 feet in diameter held. I sat down with him and showed him how to figure it out. He thanked me and left.

Alternatives. Some participants will look to you for all the alternatives and will resist suggestions that they go looking for information on their own. A few participants will challenge you about where they can find more information beyond what you provide directly and suggest as additional sources.

Some participants may choose to go on indefinitely looking for yet one more piece of information. Some do this, I believe, to avoid making a decision about what direction they want to take or how they want to solve their problem.

Still other participants will quickly become overwhelmed with alternatives and wallow in the information they have. Those wanting to search indefinitely need encouragement to stop, look, and figure out where they are—with suggestions for how to move on to transition. Those overwhelmed need help in sorting and making sense out of information they have, so they can overcome their anxiety about it.

Transition. The transition phase is the most troublesome both for the participants and for you, the teacher. Learners generally show anger, sadness, joy, great enthusiasm, profound loss, and confusion during this phase of critical thinking. Sometimes, learners will verbally attack you or other learners.

Here is where you, the teacher, must be exceedingly patient and understanding and maintain an even disposition. It is easy for you to become defensive and even angry with participants at times. This would be a normal, human reaction, but nothing would be gained.

Integration. You can help people in the integration phase by providing a kind of reality check on what they are learning and saying they now believe. You can ask questions about the practicality and the consequences of what they are suggesting. For example, a number of participants have said they are seriously considering quitting their present jobs as a result of my class or workshop. I try to help them think through the consequences of this action.

Action. A major role I play here is to help people not act on their new ideas prematurely, before they have had time to think them through completely. On the other hand, I may strongly encourage certain people, who seem to have their ideas and strategies well in hand, to act on them.

In all cases, I encourage participants, once they have acted on their new ideas and beliefs, to reflect on the action. How did it go? What would you do differently when you try this again?

Teaching critical thinking is probably the most important thing I do in my teaching. I am not merely teaching people what I know, but I am teaching them how to think and, in a profound sense, how to take charge of their own learning. I am trying to provide some insights to a more in-depth way of learning and offer enough suggestions so people can do similar critical thinking in other aspects of their lives.

CHAPTER 13

Organizing Content

Selecting proper teaching tools is a critical decision; so is organizing what you teach. Obvious reasons for carefully organizing content include: helping participants best learn the material, helping you select appropriate teaching tools, and making sure you present topics in an obvious sequence when sequence is required.

Some teachers spend little time on this. They copy the organization of a textbook, they follow the organization their teacher used when they learned the material, or they use the material they organized several years ago and haven't changed since.

WHEN TO ORGANIZE

For most classes and workshops, particularly in those areas where learners have some experience and have questions and problems, include their ideas in your organizational scheme. If you teach a five-session class that meets weekly, you might tentatively organize topics before the first session, and wait to organize more specifically after that (assuming some time at the first session is spent on identifying learner questions, interests, current knowledge, and problems).

In some content areas, particularly those where learners have little or no experience, you can organize the topics before the first session.

In my experience, no matter if I do the content organization after the first session for the remaining sessions or do the entire course organization before I begin, I find that I am constantly reorganizing content as the course or workshop moves along. Several factors cause this. Certain topics take longer than I have planned—participants have more questions, there is great interest in the topic, or several participants have difficulty understanding certain aspects of the topic. Thus I am constantly making decisions about topics. Some topics I move to succeeding sessions, some

I combine with others. I add new topics and drop others. As participants become more familiar with the content and with their own reactions to it, they will often ask for a modification of what is taught.

FACTORS TO CONSIDER

Learners' Knowledge and Experience

It is important to determine each participant's level of knowledge about the subject matter. This is particularly necessary if your group includes experienced people along with those who know little about what you are teaching. If this is the case, organize topics so you include basic, elementary material at the beginning. Inform the experienced people to consider this beginning level material as a review. You can also honestly explain that you want everyone at about the same level of understanding before you proceed. This is particularly so for most skill areas where participants must master beginning skills before they attempt those which are more advanced.

The Subject Matter

As mentioned above, many skill areas are most easily learned in a particular order, often in the sequence the skill is performed. If you are teaching snowshoeing, you would start with techniques for fastening the snowshoes to boots or shoes before teaching how to maneuver in hilly terrain or deep fresh snow.

Subject matter such as history often suggests alternative approaches for organization: by major events, by people who have made important contributions, and by chronology of happenings.

Other content, such as nonfiction book writing which I describe below, offers a wide array of approaches for organizing content.

Teacher Preference

What is most comfortable for you? What does your experience suggest? Don't overlook your preference for organizing subject matter. After all, if you are teaching the subject matter, you obviously know a great deal about it and likely have had experience applying it.

If you have taught the subject matter several times, you have learned which topics best precede other topics for particular learners in particular kinds of learning settings.

HOW TO ORGANIZE TOPICS

To illustrate one approach for organizing topics, I'll use as an example a five-session (two hours each) workshop on nonfiction book writing I teach each summer at the Rhinelander School of Arts in Rhinelander, Wisconsin. Everyone enrolled has great interest in nonfiction book writing, but usually only one or two in the class have actually written a book. So I am quite comfortable in identifying topics and doing preliminary planning before the beginning of the workshop.

Freewheeling

In my preliminary planning, I follow a procedure I call freewheeling. Others have called the same procedure mind mapping or branching (Buzan, 1974).

I base freewheeling on the idea of a wheel with a hub in the center and spokes radiating from it. It works as follows:

1. In the center of a sheet of paper write the title of your course or workshop and draw a circle around it.

2. Draw a line from the center circle and write a topic that you want to be part of your class.

3. Next, draw lines from this second circle, identifying subtopics that you want to include related to the topic. Draw circles around them as well.

4. Continue drawing both wheels from the center circle and smaller wheels until you believe you have exhausted the topics that you want to cover.

5. Occasionally, as you are drawing circles, you discover that subtopics relate to more than one main topic or that some topics really deserve to become main topics. Draw connecting lines to show these relationships.

6. Once you have a page of circles and lines, you can begin numbering the first ring of circles (main topics) in the order you want to present them in your class. Likewise, you can number the subtopics according to their order of presentation.

7. If you wish, you can go a step further and note the teaching tools that you want to consider in offering each topic.

Advantages of Freewheeling

The freewheeling approach to topic organization gives many teachers a fresh perspective on their course or workshop. Rather than having several pages comprising a typical linear outline, freewheeling starts at the core of the process (the subject you are teaching) and then works outward. Thus you are able to see your entire course or workshop on one page.

The process of making the wheels and drawing the connecting spokes encourages new topic and subtopic ideas to emerge. You will also discover new relationships between topics.

Because everything is there in front of you, as new topics emerge, you can quickly fit them onto your page. You don't have to worry about where they fit in a formal, linear outline. As you work through the process, many new topic ideas will likely appear, ideas you may never have thought about before. Freewheeling allows for their expression without restriction.

Freewheeling is a whole-brain process; ultimately it draws on both sides of your brain—the highly organized left side and the more artistic, intuitive, and creative right side.

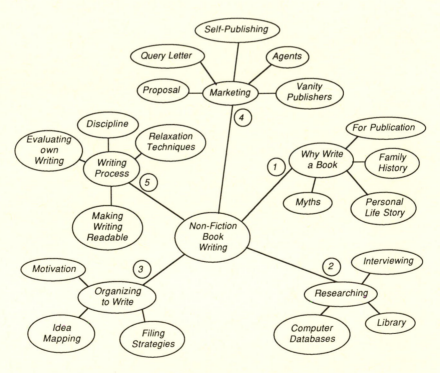

Figure 13.1

Freewheeling Example

Figure 13.1 shows a freewheeling chart I used in organizing the topics for my nonfiction writing course. I have taught this course several years, and each year I do a separate organization of topics. I include new ones and drop old ones.

During the first session of the workshop, I present a category version of my wheel on the chalkboard which includes the topics I plan to cover in the workshop. I then ask for participant reactions. I ask people to tell me which topics interest them most, which less so, and which other topics they would like to have included. After the first session I factor in this new information as I plan for succeeding sessions. Also, as I mentioned above, I make adjustments in the plan after each session.

CHAPTER 14

Making Ethical Decisions

An ethical approach to teaching concerns all of us and is a reflection of our beliefs. To overlook ethical concerns is a blatant disregard for the value of human beings and the value of what we do as teachers.

Each of us, whether we are always aware of it or not, has a set of values formed by the communities in which we grew up, as well as by our religion, social status, and ethnic background. For most of us, these factors serve as the basis for our ethical decision making.

Ethical decision making is not a skill we acquire all at once. We must constantly improve upon the process. And just as I argued that master teachers have a working philosophy for their teaching, so do they have a basis for ethical decision making.

Some of the touchstones for ethical decision making include:

- A fundamental concern for human beings
- Respect for justice and individual human rights
- Love for the earth
- Concern for quality above expediency
- Valuing a search for truth
- An appreciation of beauty

The challenge for all teachers is to search for an ethical perspective in a speed and efficiency ridden, technological, and highly competitive world. The following situations are examples of where ethical decisions often must be made.

RELATIONSHIPS WITH LEARNERS

A host of ethical situations often arise in teacher/learner relationships. Let's begin with questions emerging from the teacher/learner relationship in classes, workshops, and conferences.

Situation: Opinionated Learners

You are leading a group discussion and a participant makes a highly opinionated statement that you believe lacks a factual foundation. You begin asking the learner questions about this position and you detect the person becoming uncomfortable as the questioning proceeds.

Comments. Is it ethical to challenge participants, to help them rethink their positions, and sometimes for them to become quite uncomfortable in the process? Or the reverse, is it ethical not to challenge participants and help them move beyond where they are now, to question their positions and opinions, and to help them see new vistas?

For me, it is not only ethical to challenge participants, but I believe I have a responsibility to do so as a teacher. The key for me is the style in which I ask questions. (See the teaching tool called Questioning in Chapter 9.) I believe it is possible to critically question learners in such a way that they, although somewhat uncomfortable during the process, will appreciate it.

Situation: Personal Friendships With Learners

You develop a close personal friendship with two of the participants in your class that meets several times in the fall. You often go out for coffee with them after class. You have had them over to your house for dinner, and you have attended community social events together. You are new in the community so you welcome the friendship extended by these two participants.

Comments. Is it ethical for you to have personal friendships with learners in your classes? What are the consequences of such relationships? How do these relationships affect your relationships with participants who are not your personal friends?

For several reasons I avoid developing personal friendships with participants while they are attending my classes.

It is difficult to write an evaluation, write letters of reference, and award grades when the learner is a personal friend. Even if you argue that you are fair, some will not believe you. Why raise any question?

On the other hand, I don't believe it is ethical to maintain a cool, aloof relationship with learners, never displaying a hint of warmth or concern. The key is trying to relate to all participants in a balanced way, as difficult as this may be at times.

Situation: Learner With Personal Problem

A participant comes to your office for a conference, supposedly about a question related to your course. You notice that she is upset. She begins telling you about her husband whom she greatly fears. She shares in detail information about a recent confrontation where he has struck her and loosened two teeth.

Comments. What is an ethical response in this situation? What is ethical for you to do with this information? Is it ethical to share it with anyone?

In these situations, I usually contact my friend who heads our counseling center as to what he believes I should do. I am not qualified to deal with problems like this, except I believe I have an ethical responsibility to help the participant seek appropriate help. I may give her my friend's phone number and even make an appointment for her, if she wants me to. I try to be a good listener, but avoid giving advice. And I share this privileged information with no one, unless she wants me to help her find help.

Situation: Learners Uncomfortable With Teaching Methods

You are a teacher who uses a broad selection of teaching tools. At the completion of one of the exercises where you involved learners in creating a simulated TV show, two of the participants tell you that they were very uncomfortable during the process. One of the participants also said that she didn't believe she learned a thing during the hour her group worked on the presentation.

Comments. Is it ethical for you to use teaching tools that you know certain learners will dislike? And on the other hand, do you have a responsibility for introducing learners to teaching tools that may trigger dimensions of their learning styles with which they may not have been aware?

Is it ethical to introduce content that goes well beyond or is in someway different from what participants said they wanted based on a needs analysis? And of course the opposite, is it unethical to withhold content that you believe would assist learners even though they may not have mentioned that they wanted it?

As you might guess from my earlier comments, I believe it is appropriate and ethical to introduce learners to teaching approaches with which they are not familiar, as well as content that may seem, at first, not what they want. It is only in this way that we can help learners move beyond where they are now. I firmly believe that teachers have an ethical responsibility for helping people to become more than they are now.

Situation: Appointments With Learners

Sometimes you become extremely busy and find it difficult to keep appointments with learners. You try to call them about making a change, but sometimes you forget to do this, too.

Comments. In the area of teacher/learner relationships, one of the most ethical things you can do is keep appointments with learners. Most adult learners lead extremely busy lives that require juggling work schedules, finding a baby sitter, and making other arrangements in order to meet with you. It is never ethical to break an appointment without informing the person well ahead of time.

RELATIONSHIPS WITH OTHER TEACHERS

Situation: Comments Heard About a Fellow Teacher

You hear from several participants in your class negative comments about Joe Whiz, a fellow teacher at your institution. Learners tell you that Whiz is constantly putting them down; in fact, some say he is tyrannical in his teaching approaches. You have never cared for Whiz as a person and interact with him only when necessary. As far as you are concerned, he is not someone you want to know better. You're content to ignore him and go on with your responsibilities.

Comments. If you dislike a fellow teacher, you are certainly entitled to your opinion. Is it ever ethical to tell learners why a fellow teacher is not one of your favorite people? What if this teacher is truly a tyrant with learners? Is it then ethical to inform learners of this? Or is the appropriate ethical behavior to keep quiet and let participants find out for themselves? Is it possible that a tyrant for some learners may be viewed by other learners as a challenging, provocative instructor?

What I do when learners ask me about a teacher like Whiz is to describe his teaching style, trying to avoid making any judgment about it. I then say something like, "Some learners have found Mr. Whiz quite provocative, but you need to decide if his teaching style fits you."

TEACHING MATERIALS

As you may well know, there are certain ethical and legal considerations when copying materials from magazines, journals, and books—whatever source that may be available.

When do materials you have gleaned from many sources, reworked, rethought, and rewritten become your material and not a collection of materials assembled from multiple origins? At what point can you ethically claim the information as your own without citing the many sources?

This is an interesting question, and not easily answered. I wrestle with it all the time. A basic point to remember is that ideas cannot be copyrighted, but the way in which they are written about can. That's the legal fine point. Ethically, I try to give credit to someone else's ideas when they are clearly not mine. I will refer learners to other materials from which I have drawn pieces of my ideas, even though I have put the information together in my own way.

PROMOTIONAL MATERIALS

Situation: Marketing Director's Style

Maxwell Masters, your institution's marketing director, calls you into his office.

Masters: "Say, I've got that copy you sent over about your new course. But we've got to do some more work on it, jazz it up a little, give it a little zip, a shot of excitement."

You: "What would you like me to do?" (What is he talking about, you are thinking—overselling the course, presenting it as something different than what you have in mind? Putting you on the spot if participants don't get from the course what it says it's offering?)

Masters: "Think sales, warm bodies filling seats, write words that make people flip out their checkbooks and fill in enrollment forms. Sell a little. You teachers are all alike, too noble. You're hiding good ideas under a basket. Kick the basket away, let the ideas rise up." (He swings his arms in a broad sweeping motion.)

You: (As he talks you think—What does he really want me to do? What should I say to him? What's the ethical way for me to respond in promoting my course, and reacting to this person?) "I'll have to think about it."

Comments. Teachers often write promotional information for their courses or workshops which then appear in brochures, bulletins, and other promotional materials.

From my perspective, what the promotional material says my course or workshop will be about is what my course or workshop will be about. That doesn't mean the language describing what I plan to do can't be attractive and inviting. I have no problem with well-written promotional language that honestly says what learners should expect.

When I work with a Maxwell Masters, and there are some around (I think fewer of them in recent years), I stand my ground on honest promotion. But I also listen carefully to what marketing people have to say, and the way in which they say it. After all, if no one signs up for my course or workshop I don't have a job, and potential participants may miss an opportunity.

My oldest son, a newspaper photographer, recently signed up for what was billed as an "Advanced Course in the Techniques of Photography." The course promotion included language suggesting that here was an opportunity for professionals to further develop their skills.

To my son's dismay, he discovered the course nearly filled with people who had recently purchased cameras and were wondering how to use them. The course had been taught several times before, and word was out among the novices that this was the course to take. Word had apparently not reached the professionals that this course was improperly promoted. My son complained and, to the credit of the offering institution, got his money back.

Sometimes teachers get carried away in promoting more than they can deliver. People come with high expectations and once they are into the course or workshop they are disappointed. Their disappointment is often in two areas. What is taught turns out to be dramatically different from what the promotional materials said would be taught, or the level of the course turns out considerably different from what the promotional materials suggested.

THE TEACHER AND SOCIAL ISSUES

Many topics of interest to adults carry vast social implications and are often the seat of wide societal debate. As a teacher, are you obligated to take a neutral position and try to fairly present all sides of a question? Realistically, is it ever possible to do that? Will not your personal bias, your own feelings about the issue, show through your attempts at neutrality?

What I try to do in situations like this is to present multiple perspectives, in as balanced a way as possible, on a question or issue. But if someone asks me what my personal perspective is, I will tell them. I believe I have an ethical responsibility to present multiple perspectives on complicated issues, but I also believe I have a responsibility to myself to state what I believe.

Situation: Request From Students To Join Them in a Protest

You are teaching a four-session course on the history of the upper Mississippi River. You talk about early fur trading, you discuss the role of the Corps of Engineers in trying to maintain a uniform river depth and control flooding, you talk about attempts to protect the wildlife along the river, you talk about the development of recreational interests, and you talk about cities and villages along the river using the river as a dumping place for their wastes.

You try to present a balanced picture of what has happened on this great old river from presettlement days to the present. Several of the participants, after the third session, come to you and say they are really concerned about the river, and thank you for helping them better understand the reasons why the river has serious problems today. They want you to help them organize a protest movement to save the river's wildlife.

Comments. Many factors could influence your response. If one of the touchstones of your ethical foundation is concern for the environment, then helping participants organize a protest movement might be an appropriate response. Another approach is to say that your job as a teacher is to do just what you have done, present a balanced perspective, and if learners want to organize action groups you would not discourage them, but you would not become a part of their group either.

What decision you make is dependent on many things beyond your own beliefs. You must consider whether your employer will take kindly to a staff member becoming a lightning rod for a community issue. You must consider if your effectiveness as a teacher will decrease and whether you will alienate learners who don't agree with you.

All of these questions and more arise when you teach in areas with social consequences. Yet here is where the excitement is, and here is where teachers of adults can often truly make a difference in their communities.

RELATIONSHIP TO YOUR EMPLOYER

As suggested above, what responsibilities do you have to your employer? If your employer is clearly opposed to your taking positions on social issues and you feel strongly that you must, you have created an ethical dilemma for yourself. Are you ethically responsible first to your employer and then secondly to learners and your subject matter? Are you ethically responsible equally to employers, learners, and subject matter? Can you make short-term compromises in your ethics and still have an overall ethical position?

When does resigning your position become the ethical thing to do when you believe you can no longer support the positions taken (or not taken) by your employer? Is it the ethical thing to do to try to change your employer when you believe his or her behavior is inappropriate, or perhaps, in your mind, even unethical?

All of these are questions for which there are no easy answers, indeed no guidelines. Ethical decision making is often a lonely, individual task for each of us as we search our beliefs and values, trying to make a decision that we can live with and believe is ethically appropriate. The task is not an easy one, yet we must all constantly wrestle with ethical decision making each day that we teach.

CHAPTER 15

Assessing Quality

In the late 1970s the U.S. auto industry discovered that it could no longer sell average or low quality automobiles. The Japanese auto makers provided a quality alternative and Americans flocked to buy Toyotas, Hondas, and Nissans in record numbers. The U.S. auto manufacturers learned quickly that either they improved quality or they were out of business.

As unusual as it may sound to compare teaching adults to the auto industry, the analogy holds, I believe. Those who offer programs for adult learners can no longer merely proclaim how good they have been; they must demonstrate to adult learners that they are good *right now*. And they must demonstrate that they are good from the learner's perspective.

QUALITY QUESTIONS

In helping improve quality, let's examine questions adult learners often ask.

Will I Get My Money's Worth?

That is, compared to others offering similar courses or workshops, will I learn what I want and need to learn with this one? Will I have spent my educational dollar well? Increasingly participants will have choices. No longer will one organization, agency, or institution dominate in a community.

Will I Have Something To Say About What Is Taught?

For those topics where I have considerable experience and knowledge, will I have an opportunity to ask teachers to cover particular questions or subjects based on my interests and what I need?

121

Does the Teacher Use Stimulating and Varied Teaching Approaches?

Does the teacher recognize that participants bring a variety of preferred learning styles, and that different subject matter lends itself better to certain teaching approaches?

Is the Teacher Up-to-Date?

This doesn't necessarily mean that the teacher has a degree or an advanced degree. Formal education may certainly contribute to being up-to-date, but master teachers continue to keep up on their own, through reading, travel, short courses, visits with colleagues, and the like.

Is the Teacher Able To Relate Theory to Practice?

Another dimension to this question is the extent to which the teacher can present the abstract, general, and theoretical side of the material as well as the concrete, practical, and applied side. Ability to blend these two dimensions makes for quality teaching.

Is the Teacher Concerned About Learners as Human Beings?

Is the teacher a caring, sharing person—not a machine that wants to treat learners as so many other machines into which information is poured, and out of which learning performance is measured in carefully delineated numerical units?

Will I Be Challenged To Move Beyond Where I Am Now?

I may think I know what I want to learn, but will I, upon completion of the course or workshop, discover some new territory I had not been aware of before? This new territory may be an extension of my previous interest, but it may also be quite different from what I had been thinking before.

Will I Discover Guideposts for Continuing My Learning in This Area?

Will my teacher point me toward additional learning that I can do on my own, so I do not become dependent on formal course or workshop offerings as a sole means of meeting my learning needs and interests?

Will This Course or Workshop Contribute to Independent Learning?

Will I gain not only new knowledge and skills, but also acquire skills that I can use on my own when I want to learn something else? These skills may include how to find information and how to sort out and make sense of information, as well as how to develop critical thinking skills.

Is the Course or Workshop Convenient and Accessible?

Are courses and workshops offered at times that are convenient for me, with parking and child care? Will I have access to supplementary materials such as library resources?

Are Registration and Other Administrative Requirements Simple and at an Absolute Minimum?

Quality programs streamline these procedures and keep them at a minimum.

EVALUATION APPROACHES

A variety of specific techniques exist that can help you assess the quality of your classes and workshops. A combination of the following evaluation approaches will be helpful:

- Constantly reflect on your teaching.

- Use participant committees to assess teaching in progress.

- Use feedback from participants at the end of a course, workshop, or conference.

Take Time To Reflect

Reflecting on your teaching, including recording your reflections in a teaching journal, is an excellent way to assess how you are doing (see Chapter 3). After each workshop or class session and at the end, I take time to carefully think about what went right and what didn't. I dwell on my mistakes only long enough to figure out why they happened and what I might do to prevent them from occurring another time. I also take time to think about the teaching tools and other dimensions of the class that worked particularly well, and I try to think about why they worked well.

Adjust as You Go

Receiving feedback from learners as you teach can assist greatly in providing information about how you are doing. Such feedback can be subtle—for example, the looks learners give you when you introduce an idea. Notice the body language they use as an idea is discussed. Do they shift around and appear restless? The discussion may lack something. The kinds of questions they ask also can tell you much about how you are doing.

When I teach a class that runs for more than a half dozen sessions, at about the second session I ask the class to elect a feedback committee of three or four participants. The duties of the feedback committee are to be open to any complaints participants may have about the class ranging from my trying to cover too many ideas too quickly to not involving all the class members in the discussions. I ask the feedback committee to share with me how things are going and whatever suggestions they have for fine tuning.

I have received valuable inputs from these committees. Learners have also told me that they appreciate having a committee concerned about how things are going in the class, and having a teacher open to making adjustments as the class continues to meet.

Do an End-Of-Class Analysis

As most teachers are required to do these days, I have all participants complete an end-of-course evaluation form (see the Appendix for examples). For those courses that meet several times, I involve the feedback committee in the end-of-class evaluation process. I ask participants to complete the evaluation form during the next to last session. After the participants have filled out the forms, I give them to the feedback committee and they summarize the results. Then, as part of the last class period, I ask the feedback committee to lead a discussion of the overall evaluation of the course. This serves as the beginning place for an open discussion of the strong points of the course and where it ought to be improved.

From this open discussion I acquire information that goes well beyond what people have written on their evaluations. Having the discussion led by the feedback committee seems to make it easier for the participants to express openly how they felt about the class. In addition to discussing the strengths and what shouldn't be changed, the class also focuses on specific modifications they would like to see made. From this discussion I have learned how to restructure the class when I teach it another time, which teaching tools I should add and which I should consider dropping, changes I might consider in the pacing of the course, and which readings were particularly useful and should be continued.

For those sessions where a feedback committee is not involved, I read the evaluation forms carefully, taking into account several realities.

For some learners, filling out the form is a necessary evil and they hurriedly complete it without reflecting a great deal on their responses. In those classes where grades are recorded, some participants are reluctant to state what they really think about a course for fear of reprisal.

You, too, must be careful when reading the end-of-meeting forms and making judgments about them. Occasionally, comments from two or three participants who are critical in certain areas may be discounted with the thought, This person probably didn't understand what I was doing. That may be the case, but on the other hand, the minority opinion may be exactly what you should pay particular attention to. Even worse, some teachers, after a quick review of the forms, slip them into a file and show them to their supervisors when asked, but they don't use them as tools to help make changes in their teaching.

Often, the written comments in response to open-ended questions provide the most useful information of all. I pay particular attention to these for they often reveal the true feelings of the participant.

"Quality first" or a similar motto must be a part of our teaching, just as it has become a motto for many manufacturers in this country. Adult learners expect quality, they demand it, and they deserve it.

Appendix

Evaluation Forms

FOR EVALUATING FIRST SESSION OF A SERIES OF SESSIONS

Form A

Name of Class, Workshop _____

Date _____

    What is your overall rating of today's meeting for each of these items? Circle the appropriate number.

1 = low; 5 = high

1. Physical arrangement and comfort	1 2 3 4 5
2. Choice of methods instructor used	1 2 3 4 5
3. Participation level	1 2 3 4 5
4. Group atmosphere	1 2 3 4 5
5. What was accomplished	1 2 3 4 5
6. Interest of participants	1 2 3 4 5

Comments:

Form B

Name of class, workshop _____

Date _____

1. The three most important things we talked about today were:

   a.

   b.

   c.

2. What I learned today was:

3. A new idea for me was:

4. I'm confused about:

5. I don't understand:

6. What this session meant to me was:

END-OF-MEETING FORM FOR CLASSES THAT
MEET SEVERAL TIMES

Course Title _____

Date _____

(Circle appropriate number)

1 = standard not met

5 = standard fully met

1.	Objectives were met	1 2 3 4 5
2.	Course was logically organized	1 2 3 4 5
3.	Used time appropriately	1 2 3 4 5
4.	Assignments were useful	1 2 3 4 5
5.	Required reading was useful	1 2 3 4 5
6.	Used students' experiences well	1 2 3 4 5
7.	Grading standards were clear	1 2 3 4 5
8.	Required an appropriate amount of work	1 2 3 4 5
9.	Responded to ethnic and cultural diversity	1 2 3 4 5
10.	Evaluation activities were appropriate	1 2 3 4 5
11.	Used appropriate teaching methods	1 2 3 4 5
12.	Communicated ideas and concepts clearly	1 2 3 4 5
13.	Encouraged the free exchange of ideas	1 2 3 4 5
14.	Provided timely and thoughtful feedback	1 2 3 4 5
15.	Instructor available out of class if needed	1 2 3 4 5
16.	Instructor sensitive to student backgrounds and needs	1 2 3 4 5
17.	Demonstrated thorough and up-to-date knowledge	1 2 3 4 5
18.	Identified additional resources upon request	1 2 3 4 5
19.	Course useful in my professional development	1 2 3 4 5
20.	Course stimulating and thought provoking	1 2 3 4 5

Comments About Myself

21. I improved my understanding of concepts and
    principles   1 2 3 4 5

22. I was inspired to learn more than required   1 2 3 4 5

23. I sought help if I needed it   1 2 3 4 5

24. I completed required readings and assignments
    on time   1 2 3 4 5

25. I participated actively in class discussions and
    activities   1 2 3 4 5

26. Age: 1 = under 25; 2 = 25–35;
    3 = 36–45; 4 = 45+   1 2 3 4 5

Comments About the Course and Instructor

Comments about likes/strengths/things to be continued:

Comments about dislikes/weaknesses, things to be changed:

Other comments about your experience in this course or special gains or
value from the course:

Note: Adapted from the evaluation form used by the Department
of Continuing and Vocational Education, University of Wisconsin-
Madison

FORMS FOR WORKSHOPS, AND ONE- OR TWO-SESSION CLASSES

Name of workshop, course _____

Date _____

1. When I came to this course, I had hoped . . .

2. Now that I have taken the course, I feel . . .

3. A practical thing from the course I plan to use is . . .

4. A suggestion for improvement I would make is . . .

FORM FOR ONE-SESSION GROUP DISCUSSION

Name of Group _____

Date _____

Please circle your rating
1 = low; 5 = high

1. How satisfied were you with this session?	1 2 3 4 5
2. To what extent did you feel comfortable in the group?	1 2 3 4 5
3. To what extent did you know the group members?	1 2 3 4 5
4. To what extent were your personal objectives met?	1 2 3 4 5
5. To what extent did you contribute to the discussion?	1 2 3 4 5
6. To what extent did the group stay on the announced topic?	1 2 3 4 5
7. I would rate the group leader	1 2 3 4 5

Suggestions:

References

Apps, J. W. (1985). *Improving practice in continuing education.* San Francisco: Jossey-Bass.

Apps, J. W. (1990). *Study skills for today's college student.* New York: McGraw-Hill.

Aslanian, C. B., & Bricknell, H. M. (1980). *Americans in transition: Life changes as reasons for adult learning.* New York: College Entrance Examination Board.

Bridges, W. (1980). *Transitions.* Reading, MA: Addison-Wesley.

Buzan, T. (1974). *Use both sides of your brain.* New York: E. P. Dutton.

Cervero, R. M. (1988). *Effective continuing education for professionals.* San Francisco: Jossey-Bass.

Davies, T. (1989, October). Add humor to your teaching style; It's an attention grabber. *Adult and Continuing Education Today.* p. 8.

Delbecq, A. L., Van de Ven, A. H., & Gustafson, D. H. (1975) *Group techniques for program planning: A guide to nominal group and delphi processes.* Glenview, IL: Scott, Foresman and Company.

The entrepreneur of the decade: An interview with Steve Jobs. (1989, April). *Inc.* p. 114.

Greene, M. (1978). *Landscapes of learning.* New York: Teachers College Press, Columbia University.

Marris, M. (1974). *Loss and change.* London: Routledge & Kegan Paul.

National Association for Public Continuing and Adult Education. (1972). *Tested techniques for teachers of adults.* Washington, DC: Author.

Postman, N., & Weingartner, C. (1969). *Teaching as a subversive activity.* New York: Dell Publishing Co.

Smith, Robert M. (1982). *Learning how to learn.* Chicago: Follett.

Tom, A. R. (1984). *Teaching as a moral craft.* New York: Longman.

For Further Reading

For those of you who want to explore various aspects of teaching adults in greater depth, references in the following areas are included:

- Adult motivation
- Adult development
- Critical thinking
- Educational media
- Ethics, quality, and values
- Evaluation of teaching
- Foundations for adult learning
- Future directions
- Learning styles
- Program planning and curriculum development
- Study skills for adult learners
- Teaching professionals
- Teaching techniques

ADULT MOTIVATION

These references can help teachers understand why adults decide to participate in adult education activities, and what prompts them to learn once they sign up.

Aslanian, C. B., & Bricknell, H. M. (1980). *Americans in transition: Life changes as reasons for adult learning.* New York: College Entrance Examination Board.
Based on national research, the authors emphasize understanding the changes in people's lives as reasons for their enrolling in educational activities.

Cross, K. P. (1981). *Adults as learners: Increasing participation and facilitating learning.* San Francisco: Jossey-Bass.
Cross presents an approach for understanding adults as learners, and why they participate in education.

Maslow, A. H. (1970). *Motivation and personality* (2nd ed.) New York: Harper & Row.
Maslow emphasizes human needs as a way of understanding motivation, with self-actualization being the highest level need.

Tough, A. M. (1968) *Why adults learn: A study of the major reasons for beginning and continuing a learning project.* Toronto: Ontario Institute for Studies in Education.
The seminal study that revealed large numbers of adults participating in self-directed learning activities.

Wlodkowski, R. J. (1985). *Enhancing adult motivation to learn.* San Francisco: Jossey-Bass.

ADULT DEVELOPMENT

The following references explore various aspects of adult psychology and development.

Fowler, J. W. (1981). *Stages of faith: The psychology of human development and the quest for meaning.* San Francisco: Harper & Row.

Gilligan, C. (1982). *In a different voice: Psychological theory and women's development.* Cambridge, MA: Harvard University Press.
Adult development from a woman's perspective.

Gould, R. L. (1978). *Transformations: Growth and change in adult life.* New York: Simon & Schuster.

Havighurst, R. J. (1972). *Developmental tasks and education* (3rd ed.) New York: McKay.
This is one of the early attempts to illustrate how humans go through various stages as they live their lives, each period of time providing developmental tasks to be completed.

Knox, A. B. (1977). *Adult development and learning: A handbook on individual growth and competence in the adult years.* San Francisco: Jossey-Bass.

Levinson, D. J. (1978). *The seasons of a man's life.* New York: Knopf.
Levinson discusses adult development from a man's point of view.

Schaie, K. W., & Geiwitz, J. (1982). *Adult development and aging.* Boston: Little Brown.

Sheehy, G. (1976). *Passages.* New York: Dutton.
Here is a nontechnical, easy to read description of life stages adults face.

CRITICAL THINKING

In recent years, the need for critical thinking for all learners has become the cry of educational reformers. The following references will be useful for teachers who want to teach critical thinking techniques in adult education.

Apple, M. (1981). *Ideology and curriculum.* London: Routledge & Kegan Paul.

Apps, J. W. (1985). *Improving practice in continuing education.* San Francisco: Jossey-Bass.
Here is an approach for critically examining aspects of teaching adults.

Argyris, C. (1982). *Reasoning, learning, and action.* San Francisco: Jossey-Bass.

Brookfield, S. D. (1987). *Developing critical thinkers.* San Francisco: Jossey-Bass.

Ferguson, M. (1980). *The aquarian conspiracy.* Los Angeles: Tarcher.
This book explains how paradigm shifting occurs, and what is involved in the process from adults' perspectives.

Freire, P. (1970). *Pedagogy of the oppressed.* New York: Herder and Herder.
Freire presents concepts such as consciousness raising and praxis (relating action to reflection).

Freire, P. (1973). *Education for critical consciousness.* New York: Seabury.

Habermas, J. (1979). *Communication and the evolution of society.* Boston: Beacon Press.

Kuhn, Thomas S. (1970). *The structure of scientific revolutions*. Chicago: University of Chicago Press.
This is the classic work on what paradigm shifting is and how it occurs.

Mezirow, J. (Ed.). (1990). *Fostering critical reflection in adulthood*. San Francisco: Jossey-Bass.

Schon, D. A. (1983) *The reflective practitioner*. New York: Basic Books.
Schon explains an approach teachers can follow to look critically at what they are doing, to reflect, and to learn.

EDUCATIONAL MEDIA

For those interested in learning more about media use in teaching including, computer databases, CD-ROM, computer assisted instruction, teleconferencing, and other education media.

Ambron, S., & Hooper, K. (1988). *Interactive multimedia*. Redmond, WA: Microsoft Press.

Brand, S. (1987). *The media lab*. New York: Viking.
Here is an excellent book for becoming acquainted with teaching and learning potentials from a host of electronic media including holography, artificial intelligence, and computer uses.

Gueulette, D. (Ed.). (1982). *Microcomputers for adult learning*. Chicago: Follett.

Levin, T. K. (1987, 1988). *Teaching telecourses: Opportunities and options*. Washington, DC: The Annenberg/CPB Project.

Lewis, L. H. (Ed.). (1986). *Experiential and simulation techniques for teaching adults*. New Directions for Continuing Education, No. 30. San Francisco: Jossey-Bass.

Niemi, J. A., & Gooler, D. D. (Eds.). (1987). *Technologies for learning outside the classroom*. New Directions For Continuing Education, No. 34. San Francisco: Jossey-Bass.

Shneiderman, B., & Kearsley, G. (1989). *Hypertext hands-on*. Reading, MA: Addison-Wesley Publishing Co.

Wedemeyer, C. A. (1981). *Learning at the back door*. Madison, WI: The University of Wisconsin Press.
This is a classic text on using media and other nontraditional approaches for teaching adults.

ETHICS, QUALITY, AND VALUES

Brockett, R. G. (Ed.). (1988). *Ethical issues in adult education*. New York: Teacher's College Press.

Freedman, L. (1987). *Quality in continuing education*. San Francisco: Jossey-Bass.

Paterson, R. W. K. (1979). *Values, education and the adult*. London: Routledge & Kegan Paul.

Singarella, T., & Sork, T. (1983). Questions of values and conduct: Ethical issues for adult education. *Adult Education Quarterly*, 1983, 33, 244–251.

Tom, A. R. (1984). *Teaching as a moral craft*. New York: Longman.

EVALUATION OF TEACHING

Evaluation can take several forms, from end-of-meeting evaluation forms to considerably more sophisticated approaches for determining the value of your teaching efforts.

Eisner, E. W. (1985). *The educational imagination*. New York: Macmillan.
Eisner suggests an approach to evaluation that relies on strategies coming from the field of art.

Guba, E. G., & Lincoln, Y. S. (1981). *Effective evaluation*. San Francisco: Jossey-Bass.

Herman, J. L. (Ed.). (1988). *Program evaluation kit*. 2nd ed. Beverly Hills, CA: Sage.

Miles, M. B., & Huberman, A. M. (1984). *Qualitative data analysis*. Beverly Hills, CA: Sage.

Patton, Michael Q. (1982). *Practical evaluation*. Beverly Hills, CA: Sage.
An excellent, easy to read practical guide to evaluation strategies.

Popham, W. James. (1988). *Educational evaluation*. 2nd ed. New York: Prentice Hall, 1988.

FOUNDATIONS FOR ADULT LEARNING

These readings provide basic information necessary to fully understand the process of adult learning.

Apps, J. W. (1973). *Toward a working philosophy of adult education.* Syracuse, NY: Syracuse University Publications in Continuing Education.

Apps, J. W. (1979). *Problems in continuing education.* New York: McGraw-Hill.

Brookfield, S. D. (1986). *Understanding and facilitating adult learning.* San Francisco: Jossey-Bass.

Darkenwald, G. G., & Merriam, S. B. (1982). *Adult education: foundations of practice.* New York: Harper & Row.

Dave, R. H. (Ed.). (1976). *Foundations of lifelong education.* Elmsford, NY: Pergamon Press.

Dewey, J. (1938). *Experience and education.* New York: Collier Books.

Elias, J. L., & Merriam, S. B. (1980). *Philosophical foundations of adult education.* Malabar, FL: Krieger Publishing Company.

Greene, M. (1973). *Teacher as stranger.* Belmont, CA: Wadsworth.

Houle, C. O. (1961). *The inquiring mind: A study of the adult who continues to learn.* Madison: University of Wisconsin Press.

Houle, C. O. (1984). *Patterns of learning: New perspectives on life-span education.* San Francisco: Jossey Bass.

Kidd, J. R. (1973). *How adults learn.* New York: Cambridge Books.

Knowles, M. S. (1984). *The adult learner: A neglected species.* (3rd ed.) Houston, TX: Gulf.

Knox, A. B. (1986). *Helping adults learn.* San Francisco: Jossey-Bass.

Lindeman, E. C. (1926, 1961). *The meaning of adult education.* Montreal: Harvest House.
This is a simply written and powerful book that shows adult education in a new light. Education is life, Lindeman says.

Merriam, S. B., & Cunningham, P. M. (Eds.). (1989). *Handbook of adult education.* San Francisco: Jossey-Bass.

Mezirow, J. (1981). Critical theory of adult Learning and education. *Adult Education, 32,* 3–27.
Mezirow presents information about transformation in education while drawing on the work of Jurgen Habermas.

Miller, H. L. (1964) *Teaching and learning in adult education.* New York: Macmillan.

Postman, N. and Weingartner, C. (1969). *Teaching as a subversive activity.* New York: Dell Publishing Co.

Although somewhat dated this book raises many provocative issues relevant today.

Rogers, C. (1969). *Freedom to learn.* Columbus, Ohio: Merrill.
Rogers claims that old fashioned ways of thinking about teaching have thwarted learners' freedom to learn.

Smith, R. M. (1982). *Learning how to learn: Applied learning theory for adults.* New York: Cambridge Books.
Smith discusses the process of learning how to learn—what it means, and how people go about it.

FUTURE DIRECTIONS

The following books can be useful as you attempt to anticipate the nature of teaching adults in the years ahead. Several useful books on this topic were written many years ago.

Apps, J. W. (1988). *Higher education in a learning society.* San Francisco: Jossey-Bass.

Bryson, L. (1936) *Adult education.* New York: American Book Company.

Capra, R. (1983). *The turning point.* New York: Bantam Books.
Capra examines the future in a new light, with a new set of assumptions.

Davis, Stanley M. (1987). *Future perfect.* Reading, MA: Addison-Wesley.
Davis argues that we must focus more on prevention and strengths of learners when teaching adults rather than on problems and needs. As teachers we must help people separate what they are really interested in from they think they should be interested in, he says.

Hostler, J. (1981). *The aims of adult education.* Manchester, England: University of Manchester.

Illich, I. (1970). *Deschooling society.* New York: Harper & Row.
This is an irreverent look at present educational systems with suggestions for change.

Wurman, Richard Saul. (1989). *Information anxiety.* New York: Doubleday.
Wurman, in a highly readable book, shows how ever increasing amounts of information create information anxiety for many people.

LEARNING STYLES

To learn more about learning styles and their applications I suggest the following references.

Butler, K. A. (1984). *Learning and teaching style in theory and practice.* Maynard, MD: Gabriel Systems, Inc.
Butler discusses the Gregorc learning style inventory.

Canfield, A. A. (1980). *Learning styles inventory: Guide.* Birmingham, MI: Humanics Media.
The Canfield approach to determining learning style preference is discussed in this book.

Guild, P, B., & Garger, S. (1985). *Marching to different drummers.* Alexandria, VA: Association for Supervision and Curriculum Development.
Here is a general overview of the theory and practice related to learning style preference.

Kiersey, D., & Bates, M. (1978). *Please understand me: Character and temperament types.* Del Mar, CA: Prometheus, Nemesis.
The Myers-Briggs approach is explained in this book.

McCarthy, B. (1980). *The 4MAT system: Teaching to learning styles with right/left mode techniques.* Barrington, IL: Excell, Inc.
McCarthy explains the Kolb approach to learning style inventory.

Witkin, H., & Goodenough, D. R. (1981). *Cognitive styles: Essence and origins.* New York: International Universities Press.
The Witkin's embedded figures approach to learning styles is discussed here.

PROGRAM PLANNING AND CURRICULUM DEVELOPMENT

If you must plan programs as well as teach, you'll find the following books helpful.

Boyle, P. G. (1981). *Planning better programs.* New York: McGraw-Hill.

Cranton, P. (1989). *Planning instruction for adult learners.* Toronto: Wall and Thompson.

Delbecq, A. L., Van de Ven, A. H., & Gustafson, D. H. (1975). *Group techniques for program planning: A guide to nominal group and delphi processes.* Glenview, IL: Scott, Foresman and Company.

Houle, C. O. (1972). *The design of education.* San Francisco: Jossey-Bass.

Tyler, R. W. (1949). *Basic principles of curriculum and instruction.* Chicago: University of Chicago Press.

STUDY SKILLS FOR ADULT LEARNERS

Many times adult students will falter in their learning because of rusty or inadequate study skills. The following books are for the adult learner who wants to improve study skills.

Apps, J. W. (1982). *Improving your writing skills.* Chicago: Follett.

Apps, J. W. (1982). *Study skills for adults returning to school.* New York: McGraw-Hill.

Apps, J. W. (1990). *Study skills for today's college student.* New York: McGraw-Hill.

Bittel, B. (1990). *Adult learners survival skills.* Malabar, FL: Krieger Publishing Co.

Pauk, W. (1989). *How to study in college.* 4th ed. New York: Houghton Mifflin.

Zinsser, W. (1988). *Writing to Learn.* New York: Harper and Row.

TEACHING PROFESSIONALS

You may teach in a program where the participants are professional people continuing their education. The following books will be helpful.

Cervero, R. M. (1988). *Effective continuing education for professionals.* San Francisco: Jossey-Bass.

Houle, C. O. (1980). *Continuing learning in the professions.* San Francisco: Jossey-Bass.

Schon, D. A. (1987). *Educating the reflective practitioner.* San Francisco: Jossey-Bass.

TEACHING TECHNIQUES

These books contain practical information about a variety of teaching techniques.

Adult Education Association of the U.S.A. (1955). *How to teach adults.* Washington, DC: Author.

Adult Education Association of the U.S.A. (1955). *How to use role playing*. Washington, DC: Author.

Apps, J. W. (1972). *How to improve adult education in your church*. Minneapolis, MN: Augsburg.
This book is designed for those who teach adults in churches and other religious settings.

Apps, J. W. (1981). *The Adult Learner On Campus*. Chicago: Follett.
Here is specific information about teaching adults in college and university settings.

Boad, D., & Griffin, V. (1987). *Appreciating adults learning*. London: Kogan Page.

Bock, L. A. (1979). *Teaching adults in continuing education*. Champaign-Urbana: Office of Continuing Education and Public Service, University of Illinois.

Bridges, W. (1980). *Transitions*. Reading, MA: Addison-Wesley.
Bridges describes how adults wrestle with the transitions that occur as they learn and grow.

Daloz, L. A. (1986). *Effective teaching and mentoring*. San Francisco: Jossey-Bass.

Dickinson, G. (1973). *Teaching adults: A handbook for instructors*. Toronto: New Press.

Draves, W. A. (1984). *How to teach adults*. Manhattan, KS: Learning Resources Network.
A good, basic starting text for those new to teaching adults.

Eble, K. E. (1976). *The craft of teaching*. San Francisco: Jossey-Bass.
Eble's focus is on higher education but many applications can be made to teaching adults in other educational settings and levels.

Gagne, R. M. (1977). *The conditions of learning*. (3rd ed.) New York: Holt Rinehart and Winston.
This book describes a behavioral objectives approach to teaching adults.

Galbraith, M. W. (Ed.) (1989). *Adult learning methods*. Malabar, FL: Krieger Publishing Co.

Galbraith, M. W. (Ed.) (1990). *Facilitating adult learning: A transactional process*. Malabar, FL: Krieger Publishing Co.

Hayes, E. (Ed.). (1989). *Effective teaching styles*. New Directions for Continuing Education, No. 43. San Francisco: Jossey-Bass.

Knowles, M. S. (1980). *The modern practice of adult education: From pedagogy to andragogy* (2nd Ed.). New York: Cambridge Books.
     Knowles emphasizes how adults are different from children, and illustrates teaching approaches to facilitate adult learning. He explains the concept of andragogy.

McKeachie, W. J. (1978). *Teaching tips: A guidebook for the beginning college teacher*. Lexington, Mass: D. C. Heath and Company.
     A standard guidebook for scores of college teachers; many of the suggestions apply to teaching adults.

National Association of Public School Adult Educators. (1959). *When you're teaching adults*. Washington, DC: Author.

Robinson, R. D. (1979). *Helping adults learn and change*. Milwaukee, WI: Omnibook.

Seaman, D. F., & Fellenz, R. A. (1989). *Effective strategies for teaching adults*. Columbus, OH: Merrill Publishing Company.

Snyder, R. E., & Ulmer, C. (1972). *Guide to teaching techniques for adult classes*. Englewood Cliffs, NJ: Prentice-Hall.

Sork, R. J. (Ed.). (1984). *Designing and implementing effective workshops*. New Directions for Continuing Education, No. 22. San Francisco: Jossey-Bass.

Stenzel, Anne K., & Feeney, Helen, M. (1970). *Learning by the case method*. New York: Seabury Press.

INDEX